# Anything For a Quiet Life by John Webster

## Written with Thomas Middleton

John Webster is known primarily for his two Jacobean tragedies, The Duchess of Malfi and The White Devil. Much of the detail and chronology of his life that led to these two pivotal works is, however, unknown.

His father, a carriage maker also named John Webster, married a blacksmith's daughter, Elizabeth Coates, on November 4th, 1577, and it is likely that Webster was born within a year or two in or near London.

The family lived in St. Sepulchre's parish. Both his father and his uncle, Edward Webster, were Freemen of the Merchant Taylors' Company and Webster attended Merchant Taylors' School in Suffolk Lane, London.

Some accounts say he began to study law but nothing is certain although there are some legal aspects to his later works to suggest this may have been so.

By 1602, Webster was employed working as part of various teams of playwrights on history plays, though unfortunately most were never printed and therefore do not survive. These include a tragedy Caesar's Fall (written with Michael Drayton, Thomas Dekker, Thomas Middleton and Anthony Munday), and a collaboration with Thomas Dekker; Christmas Comes but Once a Year (1602). This factory line assembly of plays may seem rather odd to us today but plays then ran for much shorter durations and consequently a steady supply had to be assured.

Webster's relationship with Dekker seems to have been a good one. Together they wrote Sir Thomas Wyatt, printed in 1607, although it is thought first performed in 1602 and two city comedies, Westward Ho! in 1604 and Northward Ho! in 1605. It seems Webster also adapted, in 1604, John Marston's The Malcontent for staging by the King's Men.

On March 18th, 1606 Webster married the 17-year-old Sara Peniall at St Mary's Church, Islington. Sara was 7 months pregnant and marrying during Lent required the issuing of a special permit, hence the certainty of the date. Their first child, John, was baptised at the parish of St Dunstan-in-the-West on March 8th, 1606. Records show that on the death of a neighbour, who died in 1617, several bequests were made to the Webster family and it is therefore thought that other children were born to the couple.

Despite his ability to write comedy, and to collaborate with others, Webster is remembered best for his sole authorship on two brooding English tragedies based on Italian sources. The White Devil, retells the intrigues involving Vittoria Accoramboni, an Italian woman assassinated at the age of 28. It was performed at the open-air Red Bull Theatre in 1612 but was unsuccessful, perhaps being too high brow for a working-class audience.

In 1614 The Duchess of Malfi was first performed by the King's Men, most probably in the indoor Blackfriars Theatre and to a more high-brow audience. It proved to be more successful.

The play Guise, based on French history, was also written but him but no text has survived.

Webster wrote one more play on his own: The Devil's Law Case (c. 1617–1619), a tragicomedy.

He continued to write thereafter but always in collaboration and usually city comedies; Anything for a Quiet Life (c. 1621), with Thomas Middleton, and A Cure for a Cuckold (c. 1624), with William Rowley.

In 1624, he also co-wrote a topical play about a recent scandal, Keep the Widow Waking (with John Ford, Rowley and Dekker). The play itself is lost, although its plot is known from a court case.

There is also some certainty that he contributed to the tragicomedy The Fair Maid of the Inn with John Fletcher, John Ford, and Phillip Massinger. His Appius and Virginia, was probably written with Thomas Heywood, and is of uncertain date.

It is believed, mainly from Thomas Heywood's Hierarchie of the Blessed Angels (licensed 7 November 1634) that speaks of him in the past tense that John Webster had died at some point in that year of 1634.

## Thomas Middleton

Thomas Middleton was born in London in April 1580 and baptised on 18th April.

Middleton was aged only five when his father died. His mother remarried but this unfortunately fell apart into a fifteen year legal dispute regarding the inheritance due Thomas and his younger sister.

By the time he left Oxford, at the turn of the Century, Middleton had and published Microcynicon: Six Snarling Satirese which was denounced by the Archbishop of Canterbury and publicly burned.

In the early years of the 17th century, Middleton wrote topical pamphlets. One – Penniless Parliament of Threadbare Poets was reprinted several times and the subject of a parliamentary inquiry.

These early years writing plays continued to attract controversy. His writing partnership with Thomas Dekker brought him into conflict with Ben Jonson and George Chapman in the so-called War of the Theatres.

His finest work with Dekker was undoubtedly The Roaring Girl, a biography of the notorious Mary Frith.

In the 1610s, Middleton began another playwriting partnership, this time with the actor William Rowley, producing another slew of plays including Wit at Several Weapons and A Fair Quarrel.

The ever adaptable Middleton seemed at ease working with others or by himself. His solo writing credits include the comic masterpiece, A Chaste Maid in Cheapside, in 1613.

In 1620 he was officially appointed as chronologer of the City of London, a post he held until his death.

The 1620s saw the production of his and Rowley's tragedy, and continual favourite, The Changeling, and of several other tragicomedies.

However in 1624, he reached a peak of notoriety when his dramatic allegory A Game at Chess was staged by the King's Men. Though Middleton's approach was strongly patriotic, the Privy Council silenced the play after only nine performances at the Globe theatre, having received a complaint from the Spanish ambassador.

What happened next is a mystery. It is the last play recorded as having being written by Middleton.

Thomas Middleton died at his home at Newington Butts in Southwark in the summer of 1627, and was buried on July 4th, in St Mary's churchyard which today survives as a public park in Elephant and Castle.

## Acts and Scenes

Dramatis Personae
Lord BEAUFORT
SIR FRANCIS Cressingham, an alchemist
OLD FRANKLIN, a country gentleman
George CRESSINGHAM, son to Sir Francis
FRANKLIN, a sea captain, son to Old Franklin, and companion to George Cressingham
Master Water CHAMLET, a citizen
KNAVESBEE, a lawyer, and pander to his wife
SAUNDER, steward to Sir Francis

GEORGE and RALPH, two prentices to Water Chamlet
A SURVEYOR
Sweetball, a BARBER
Toby, the Barber's BOY
FLESHHOOK and COUNTERBUFF, a sergeant and a yeoman
MARIA and EDWARD, two children of Sir Francis Cressingham, nurs'd by Water Chamlet
Three CREDITORS named Pennystone, Phillip, and Cheyney
LADY CRESSINGHAM, wife to Sir Francis
MISTRESS CRESSINGHAM, wife to George Cressingham, disguised as Selenger, page to Lord Beaufort
RACHEL, wife to Water Chamlet
SIB, Knavesbee's wife
MARGARITA, a French bawd

PROLOGUE

Howe'er th' intents and appetites of men
Are different as their faces, how and when
T' employ their actions, yet all without strife
Meet in this point: Anything for a Quiet Life.
Nor is there one, I think, that's hither come
For his delight, but would find peace at home
On any terms. The lawyer does not cease
To talk himself into a sweat without pain,
And so his fees buy quiet, 'tis his gain:
The poor man does endure the scorching sun,
And feels no weariness, his day-labour done,
So his wife entertain him with a smile,
And thank his travail, though she slept the while.
This being in men of all conditions true,
Does give our play a name; and if to you
It yield content, and usual delight,
For our parts we shall sleep secure tonight.

ACT I

SCENE I - Sir Francis Cressingham's House

Enter the **LORD BEAUFORT** and **SIR FRANCIS CRESSINGHAM**.

**BEAUFORT**
Away, I am asham'd of your proceedings,
And, seriously, you have in this one act
Overthrown the reputation the world
Held of your wisdom.

**SIR FRANCIS**
Why, sir?

**BEAUFORT**
Can you not see
Your error? That having buried so good a wife
Not a month since, one that—to speak the truth,
Had all those excellencies which our books
Have only feign'd to make a complete wife,
Most exactly in her in practice—and to marry
A girl of fifteen, one bred up i' th' court,
That by all consonancy of reason, is like
To cross your estate. Why, one new gown of hers,
When 'tis paid for, will eat you out of the keeping
Of a bountiful Christmas. I am asham'd of you,
For you shall make too dear a proof of it,
I fear, that in the election of a wife,
As in a project of war, to err but once
Is to be undone forever.

**SIR FRANCIS**
Good my lord,
I do beseech you let your better judgment
Go along with your reprehension.

**BEAUFORT**
So it does,
And can find nought to extenuate your fault,
But your dotage: you are a man well sunk in years,
And to graft such a young blossom into your stock,
Is the next way to make every carnal eye
Bespeak your injury. Troth, I pity her too;
She was not made to wither and go out
By painted fires, that yields her no more heat
Than to be lodg'd in some bleak banqueting house
I' th' dead of winter. And what follows then?
Your shame, and the ruin of your children, and there's
The end of a rash bargain.

**SIR FRANCIS**
With your pardon,
That she is young is true; but that discretion
Has gone beyond her years, and overta'en
Those of maturer age, does more improve
Her goodness. I confess she was bred at court,
But so retiredly, that as still the best
In some place is to be learnt there, so her life
Did rectify itself more by the court chapel

Than by the office of the revels; best of all virtues
Are to be found at court, and where you meet
With writings contrary to this known truth,
They are framed by men that never were so happy
To be planted there to know it: for the difference
Between her youth and mine, if you will read
A matron's sober staidness in her eye,
And all the other grave demeanour fitting
The governess of a house, you'll then confess
There's no disparity between us.

[Enter **MASTER WATER CHAMLET**.

**BEAUFORT**
Come, come, you read
What you would her to be, not what she is.
Oh, Master Water Chamlet, you are welcome.

**CHAMLET**
I thank your lordship.

**BEAUFORT**
And what news stirring in Cheapside?

**CHAMLET**
Nothing new there, my lord, but the Standard.

**BEAUFORT**
Oh, that's a monument your wives take great delight in; I do hear you are grown a mighty purchaser. I hope shortly to find you a continual resident upon the north aisle of the Exchange.

**CHAMLET**
Where? With the Scotchmen?

**BEAUFORT**
No, sir, with the aldermen.

**CHAMLET**
Believe it, I am a poor commoner.

**SIR FRANCIS**
Come, you are warm, and blest with a fair wife.

**CHAMLET**
There's it: her going brave has the only virtue to improve my credit in the subsidy book.

**BEAUFORT**
But I pray, how thrives your new plantation of silkworms, those I saw last summer at your garden?

**CHAMLET**
They are remov'd, sir.

**BEAUFORT**
Whither?

**CHAMLET**
This winter my wife has remov'd them home to a fair chamber, where diverse courtiers use to come and see them, and my wife carries them up; I think shortly, what with the store of visitants, they'll prove as chargeable to me as the morrow after Simon and Jude, only excepting the taking down and setting up again of my glass windows.

**BEAUFORT**
That a man of your estate should be so gripple-minded, and repining at his wife's bounty!

**SIR FRANCIS**
There are no such ridiculous things i' th' world as those love money better than themselves; for though they have understanding to know riches, a mind to seek them, and a wit to find them, and policy to keep them, and long life to possess them, yet commonly they have withal such a false sight, such blear'd eyes, all their wealth when it lies before them does seem poverty, and such a one are you.

**CHAMLET**
Good Sir Francis, you have had sore eyes too: you have been a gamester, but you have given it o'er, and to redeem the vice belong'd to't, now you entertain certain parcels of silenc'd ministers, which I think will equally undo you. Yet should these waste you but lenitively, your devising new watermills for recovery of drown'd land, and certain dreams you have in alchemy to find the philosopher's stone, will certainly draw you to th' bottom. I speak freely, sir, and would not have you angry, for I love you.

**SIR FRANCIS**
I am deeply in your books for furnishing my late wedding. Have you brought a note of the particulars?

**CHAMLET**
No, sir; at more leisure.

**SIR FRANCIS**
What comes the sum to?

**CHAMLET**
For tissue, cloth of gold, velvets and silks, about fifteen hundred pounds.

**SIR FRANCIS**
Your money is ready.

**CHAMLET**
Sir, I thank you.

**SIR FRANCIS**

And how does my two young children, whom I have put to board with you?

**BEAUFORT**
Have you put forth two of your children already?

**SIR FRANCIS**
'Twas my wife's discretion to have it so.

**BEAUFORT**
Come, 'tis the first principle in a mother-in-law's chop-logic to divide the family, to remove from forth your sight the objects that her cunning knows would dull her insinuation. Had you been a kind father, it would have been your practice every day to have preach'd to these two young ones carefully your late wife's funeral sermon. 'Las, poor souls, are they turn'd so soon a-grazing?

[Enter **GEORGE CRESSINGHAM** and **FRANKLIN**.

**CHAMLET**
My lord, they are plac'd where they shall be respected as mine own.

**BEAUFORT**
I make no question of it, good Master Chamlet.
[To **SIR FRANCIS**] See here your eldest son, Cressingham.

**SIR FRANCIS**
You have displeas'd and griev'd your mother-in-law,
And till you have made submission and procur'd
Her pardon, I'll not know you for my son.

**CRESSINGHAM**
I have wrought her no offense, sir. The difference
Grew about certain jewels which my mother,
By your consent, lying upon her deathbed,
Bequeath'd to her three children; these I demanded,
And being denied these, thought this sin of hers,
To violate so gentle a request
Of her predecessor, was an ill foregoing
Of a mother-in-law's harsh nature.

**SIR FRANCIS**
Sir, understand
My will mov'd in her denial: you have jewels,
To pawn or sell them. Sirrah, I will have you
As obedient to this woman as to myself;
Till then, you are none of mine.

**CHAMLET**
Oh, Master George,
Be rul'd, do anything for a quiet life!

Your father's peace of life moves in it too.
I have a wife: when she is in the sullens,
Like a cook's dog that you see turn a wheel,
She will be sure to go and hide herself
Out of the way dinner and supper, and in
These fits Bow Bell is a still organ to her.
When we were married first, I well remember,
Her railing did appear but a vision,
Till certain scratches on my hand and face
Assur'd me it was substantial. She's a creature
Uses to waylay my faults, and more desires
To find them out than to have them amended.
She has a book, which I may truly nominate
Her Black Book, for she remembers in it
In short items all my misdemeanours,

As: Item, such a day I was got fox'd with foolish metheglin in the company of certain Welsh chapmen; item, such a day being at the Artillery Garden, one of my neighbours in courtesy to salute me with his musket, set afire my fustian-and-apes breeches; such a day I lost fifty pound in hugger-mugger at dice in the quest-house; item, I lent money to a sea captain on his bare "Confound him, he would pay me again the next morning," and such like,

For which she rail'd upon me when I should sleep,
And that's, you know, intolerable, for indeed
'Twill tame an elephant.

**CRESSINGHAM**
'Tis a shrewd vexation,
But your discretion, sir, does bear it out
With a month's sufferance.

**CHAMLET**
Yes, and I would wish you
To follow mine example.

**FRANKLIN**
Here's small comfort,
George, from your father: here's a lord whom I
Have long depended upon for employment; I will see
If my suit will thrive better. [To **BEAUFORT**] Please your lordship,
You know I am a younger brother, and my fate,
Throwing me upon the late ill-starr'd voyage
To Guiana, failing of our golden hopes,
I and my ship address'd ourselves to serve
The duke of Florence.

**BEAUFORT**
Yes, I understood it so.

**FRANKLIN**
Who gave me both encouragement and means
To do him some small service 'gainst the Turk;
Being settled there, both in his pay and trust,
Your lordship, minding to rig forth a ship
To trade for the East Indies, sent for me,
And what your promise was, if I would leave
So great a fortune to become your servant,
Your letters yet can witness.

**BEAUFORT**
Yes, what follows?

**FRANKLIN**
That for aught I perceive, your former purpose
Is quite forgotten: I have stayed here two months
And find your intended voyage but a dream,
And the ship you talk of as imaginary,
As that the astronomers point at in the clouds.
I have spent two thousand ducats since my arrival;
Men that have command, my lord, at sea cannot live
Ashore without money.

**BEAUFORT**
Know, sir, a late purchase
Which cost me a great sum has diverted me
From my former purpose; besides, suits in law
Do every term so trouble me by land,
I have forgot going by water. If you please
To rank yourself among my followers,
You shall be welcome, and I'll make your means
Better than any gentleman's I keep.

**FRANKLIN**
Some twenty mark a year! Will that maintain
Scarlet and gold lace, play at th' ordinary,
And bevers at the tavern?

**BEAUFORT**
I had thought
To prefer you to have been captain of a ship
That's bound for the Red Sea.

**FRANKLIN**
What hinders it?

**BEAUFORT**

Why, certainly, the merchants are possess'd
You have been a pirate.

**FRANKLIN**
Say I were one still,
If I were past the Line once, why methinks
I should do them better service.

[Enter **KNAVESBEE**.

**BEAUFORT**
Pray, forbear.
Here's a gentleman whose business
Must engross me wholly.

[**CRESSINGHAM** takes **FRANKLIN** aside as **BEAUFORT** and **KNAVESBEE** talk.

**CRESSINGHAM**
What's he? Dost thou know him?

**FRANKLIN**
A pox upon him! A very knave and rascal
That goes a-hunting with the penal statutes;
And good for nought but to persuade their lords
To rack their rents, and give o'er housekeeping.
Such caterpillars may hang at their lord's ears
When better men are neglected.

**CRESSINGHAM**
What's his name?

**FRANKLIN**
Knavesbee.

**CRESSINGHAM**
Knavesbee!

**FRANKLIN**
One that deals in a tenth share
About projections: he and his partners, when
They have got a suit once past the seal, will so
Wrangle about partition, and sometimes
They fall to th' ears about it, like your fencers,
That cudgel one another by patent; you shall see him
So terribly bedash'd in a Michaelmas term
Coming from Westminster, that you would swear
He were lighted from a horse race. Hang him, hang him!
He's a scurvy informer; h'as more cozenage in him

Than is in five travelling lotteries.
To feed a kite with the carrion of this knave
When he's dead, and reclaim her, oh, she would prove
An excellent hawk for talon! H'as a fair creature
To his wife too, and a witty rogue it is,
And some men think this knave will wink at small faults.
But, honest George, what shall become of us now?

**CRESSINGHAM**
Faith, I am resolv'd to set up my rest
For the Low Countries.

**FRANKLIN**
To serve there?

**CRESSINGHAM**
Yes, certain.

**FRANKLIN**
There's thin commons; besides, they have added one day
More to th' week than was in the creation.
Art thou valiant? Art thou valiant, George?

**CRESSINGHAM**
I may be, and I be put to't.

**FRANKLIN**
O never fear that;
Thou canst not live two hours after thy landing
Without a quarrel. Thou must resolve to fight,
Or, like a sumner, thou'lt be bastanado'd
At every town's end. You shall have gallants there
As ragged as the fall o' th' leaf, that live
In Holland, where the finest linen's made,
And yet wear ne'er a shirt. These will not only
Quarrel with a newcomer when they are drunk,
But they will quarrel with any man has means
To be drunk afore them. Follow my council, George,
Thou shalt not go o'er; we'll live here i' th' city.

**CRESSINGHAM**
But how?

**FRANKLIN**
How? Why, as other gallants do
That feed high, and play copiously, yet brag
They have but nine pound a year to live on. These have wit
To turn rich fools and gulls into quarter-days,

That bring them in certain payment. I have a project
Reflects upon yon merchant, Master Chamlet,
Shall put us into money.

**CRESSINGHAM**
What is't?

**FRANKLIN**
Nay,
I will not stale it aforehand; 'tis a new one.
Nor cheating amongst gallants may seem strange;
Why, a reaching wit goes current on th' Exchange.

[Exeunt **GEORGE CRESSINGHAM** and **FRANKLIN**.

**KNAVESBEE**
O my lord, I remember you and I were students together at Cambridge; but believe me, you went far
beyond me.

**BEAUFORT**
When I studied there, I had so fantastical a brain, that like a felfare, frighted in winter by a birding-piece,
I could settle nowhere: here and there a little of every several art, and away.

**KNAVESBEE**
Now my wit, though it were more dull, yet I went slowly on, and as diverse others, when I could not
prove an excellent scholar, by a plodding patience I attain'd to be a petty lawyer; and I thank my
dullness for't. You may stamp in lead any figure, but in oil or quicksilver nothing can be imprinted, for
they keep no certain station.

**BEAUFORT**
O, you tax me well of irresolution; but say, worthy friend, how thrives my weighty suit which I have
trusted to your friendly bosom? Is there any hope to make me happy?

**KNAVESBEE**
'Tis yet questionable, for I have not broke the ice to her; an hour hence come to my house, and if it lie in
man, be sure, as the law phrase says, I will create you lord paramount of your wishes.

**BEAUFORT**
O my best friend, and one that takes the hardest course i' th' world to make himself so!

[Exit **KNAVESBEE**.

Sir, now I'll take my leave.

**SIR FRANCIS**
Nay, good my lord; my wife is coming down.

[Enter **LADY CRESSINGHAM** and **SAUNDER**.

**BEAUFORT**
Pray, pardon me, I have business so importunes me o' th' sudden, I cannot stay; deliver mine excuse, and in your ear this: let not a fair woman make you forget your children.

[Exit.

**LADY CRESSINGHAM**
What? Are you taking leave too?

**CHAMLET**
Yes, good madam.

**LADY CRESSINGHAM**
The rich stuffs which my husband bought of you, the works of them are too common. I have got a Dutch painter to draw patterns, which I'll have sent to your factors, as in Italy, at Florence and Ragusa, where these stuffs are woven, to have pieces made for mine own wearing of a new invention.

**CHAMLET**
You may, lady, but 'twill be somewhat chargeable.

**LADY CRESSINGHAM**
Chargeable! What of that? If I live another year, I'll have my agents shall lie for me at Paris, and at Venice, and at Valladolid in Spain, for intelligence of all new fashions.

**SIR FRANCIS**
Do, sweetest; thou deserv'st to be exquisite in all things.

**CHAMLET**
The two children to which you are mother-in-law would be repaired too; 'tis time they had new clothing.

**LADY CRESSINGHAM**
I pray, sir, do not trouble me with them;
They have a father indulgent and careful of them.

**SIR FRANCIS**
I am sorry you made the motion to her.

**CHAMLET**
I have done.
[Aside] He has run himself into a pretty dotage.—
Madam, with your leave.
[Aside] He's tied to a new law and a new wife,
Yet to my old proverb, "Anything for a Quiet Life."

[Exit **CHAMLET**.

**LADY CRESSINGHAM**

Good friend, I have a suit to you.

**SIR FRANCIS**
Dearest self, you most powerfully sway me.

**LADY CRESSINGHAM**
That you would give o'er this fruitless, if I may not say this idle, study of alchemy; why, half your house looks like a glass-house.

**SAUNDER**
And the smoke you make is a worse enemy to good housekeeping than tobacco.

**LADY CRESSINGHAM**
Should one of your glasses break, it might bring you to a dead palsy.

**SAUNDER**
My lord, your quicksilver has made all your more solid gold and silver fly in fume.

**SIR FRANCIS**
I'll be rul'd by you in anything.

**LADY CRESSINGHAM**
Go, Saunder, break all the glasses.

**SAUNDER**
I fly to't.

[Exit **SAUNDER**.

**LADY CRESSINGHAM**
Why, noble friend, would you find the true philosopher's stone indeed, my good housewifery should do it. You understand I was bred up with a great courtly lady; do not think all women mind gay clothes and riot: there are some widows living have improv'd both their own fortunes and their children's. Would you take my counsel, I'd advise you to sell your land.

**SIR FRANCIS**
My land!

**LADY CRESSINGHAM**
Yes, and the manor house upon't: 'tis rotten. Oh, the new-fashion'd buildings brought from the Hague: 'tis stately! I have intelligence of a purchase, and the title sound, will for half the money you may sell yours for, bring you in more rent than yours now yields you.

**SIR FRANCIS**
If it be so good a pennyworth, I need not sell my land to purchase it: I'll procure money to do it.

**LADY CRESSINGHAM**
Where, sir?

**SIR FRANCIS**
Why, I'll take it up at interest.

**LADY CRESSINGHAM**
Never did any man thrive that purchas'd with use-money.

**SIR FRANCIS**
How come you to know these thrifty principles?

**LADY CRESSINGHAM**
How? Why, my father was a lawyer, and died in the commission, and may not I by a natural instinct have a reaching that way? There are, on mine own knowledge, some divines' daughters infinitely affected with reading controversies, and that, some think, has been a means to bring so many suits into the spiritual court. Pray, be advised, sell your land, and purchase more: I knew a peddlar by being merchant this way, is become lord of many manors. We should look to lengthen our estates as we do our lives;

[Enter **SAUNDER.**

And though I am young, yet I am confident
Your able constitution of body
When you are past fourscore, shall keep you fresh
Till I arrive at the neglected year
That I am past childbearing, and yet even there
Quick'ning our faint heats in a soft embrace,
And kindling divine flames in fervent prayers,
We may both go out together, and one tomb
Quit our executors the rites of two.

**SIR FRANCIS**
Oh, you are so wise and so good in everything:
I move by your direction.

**SAUNDER** [Aside]
She has caught him!

[Exeunt.

ACT II

SCENE I - Knavesbee's House

Enter **KNAVESBEE** and his wife, **SIB.** Table.

**KNAVESBEE**
Have you drunk the eggs and muscadine I sent you?

**SIB**
No, they are too fulsome.

**KNAVESBEE**
Away, y'are a fool!
[Aside] How shall I begin to break the matter to her?—
I do long, wife.

**SIB**
Long, sir?

**KNAVESBEE**
Long infinitely.
Sit down; there is a penitential motion in me,
Which if thou wilt but second, I shall be
One of the happiest men in Europe.

**SIB**
What might that be?

**KNAVESBEE**
I had last night one of the strangest dreams;
Methought I was thy confessor, thou mine,
And we reveal'd between us privately
How often we had wrong'd each other's bed
Since we were married.

**SIB**
Came you drunk to bed?
There was a dream with a witness!

**KNAVESBEE**
No, no witness.
I dreamt nobody heard it but we two.
This dream, wife, do I long to put in act:
Let us confess each other, and I vow
Whatever thou hast done with that sweet corpse
In the way of natural frailty, I protest
Most freely I will pardon.

**SIB**
Go sleep again!
Was there ever such a motion?

**KNAVESBEE**
Nay, sweet woman,
And thou wilt not have me run mad with my desire,

Be persuaded to't.

**SIB**
Well, be it your pleasure.

**KNAVESBEE**
But to answer truly.

**SIB**
O, most sincerely!

**KNAVESBEE**
Begin then: examine me first.

**SIB**
Why, I know not what to ask you.

**KNAVESBEE**
Let me see. Your father was a captain: demand of me how many dead pays I am to answer for in the muster-book of wedlock, by the martial fault of borrowing from my neighbours.

**SIB**
Troth, I can ask no such foolish questions.

**KNAVESBEE**
Why then, open confession I hope, dear wife, will merit freer pardon: I sinn'd twice with my laundress, and last circuit there was at Banbury a she-chamberlain that had a spice of purity, but at last I prevailed over her.

**SIB**
O, you are an ungracious husband!

**KNAVESBEE**
I have made a vow never to ride abroad but in thy company. Oh, a little drink makes me clamber like a monkey! Now, sweet wife, you have been an outlier too: which is best feed, in the forest or in the purlieus?

**SIB**
A foolish mind of you i' this!

**KNAVESBEE**
Nay, sweet love, confess freely; I have given you the example.

**SIB**
Why, you know I went last year to Sturbridge Fair.

**KNAVESBEE**
Yes.

**SIB**

And being in Cambridge, a handsome scholar, one of Emmanuel College, fell in love with me.

**KNAVESBEE**

O, you sweet-breath'd monkey!

**SIB**

Go hang, you are so boisterous!

**KNAVESBEE**

But did this scholar show thee his chamber?

**SIB**

Yes.

**KNAVESBEE**

And didst thou like him?

**SIB**

Like him! Oh, he had the most enticing'st straw-colour'd beard, a woman with black eyes would have lov'd him like jet! He was the finest man, with a formal wit; and he had a fine dog that sure was whelp'd i' th' college, for he understood Latin.

**KNAVESBEE**

Pooh waw! This is nothing till I know what he did in's chamber.

**SIB**

He burnt wormwood in't to kill the fleas i' th' rushes.

**KNAVESBEE**

But what did he to thee there?

**SIB**

Some five-and-twenty years hence I may chance tell you. Fie upon you! What tricks, what crotchets are these? Have you plac'd anybody behind the arras to hear my confession? I heard one in England got a divorce from's wife by such a trick; were I dispos'd now, I would make you as mad. You shall see me play the changeling.

**KNAVESBEE**

No, no, wife, you shall see me play the changeling: hadst thou confess'd, this other suit I'll now prefer to thee would have been dispatch'd in a trice.

**SIB**

And what's that, sir?

**KNAVESBEE**

Thou wilt wonder at it four-and-twenty years longer than nine days.

**SIB**
I would very fain hear it.

**KNAVESBEE**
There is a lord o' th' court, upon my credit, a most dear, honourable friend of mine, that must lie with thee. Do you laugh? 'Tis not come to that; you'll laugh when you know who 'tis.

**SIB**
Are you stark mad?

**KNAVESBEE**
On my religion, I have past my word for't.
'Tis the Lord Beaufort: thou art made happy forever!
The generous and bountiful Lord Beaufort!
You being both so excellent, 'twere pity
If such rare pieces should not be conferred
And sampled together.

**SIB**
Do you mean seriously?

**KNAVESBEE**
As I hope for preferment.

**SIB**
And can you lose me thus?

**KNAVESBEE**
Lose you! I shall love you the better! Why, what's the viewing any wardrobe or jewel-house without a companion to confer their likings? Yet now I view thee well, methinks thou art a rare monopoly, and great pity one man should enjoy thee.

**SIB**
This is pretty!

**KNAVESBEE**
Let's divorce ourselves so long, or think I am gone to th' Indies, or lie with him when I am asleep, for some Familists of Amsterdam will tell you it may be done with a safe conscience. Come, you wanton, what hurt can this do to you? I protest nothing so much as to keep company with an old woman has sore eyes: no more wrong than I do my beaver when I try it thus.

[He rubs it against the fur, then smoothes it.]

Look, this is all: smooth, and keeps fashion still.

**SIB**
You are one of the basest fellows.

**KNAVESBEE**
I look'd for chiding;
I do make this a kind of fortitude
The Romans never dreamt of: and 'twere known,
I should be spoke and writ of when I am rotten,
For 'tis beyond example.

**SIB**
But, I pray, resolve me:
Suppose this done, could you ever love me after?

**KNAVESBEE**
I protest I never thought so well of thee
Till I knew he took a fancy to thee, like one
That has variety of choice meat before him,
Yet has no stomach to't until he hear
Another praise.

[Knock within.

Hark, my lord is coming.

**SIB**
Possible!

**KNAVESBEE**
And my preferment comes along with him. Be wise, mind your good, and to confute all reason in the world which thou canst urge against it. When 'tis done, we will be married again, wife, which some say is the only supersedeas about Limehouse to remove cuckoldry.

[Enter **BEAUFORT**.

**BEAUFORT**
Come, are you ready to attend me to the court?

**KNAVESBEE**
Yes, my lord.

**BEAUFORT**
Is this fair one your wife?

**KNAVESBEE**
At your lordship's service. I will look up some writings and return presently.

[Exit **KNAVESBEE**.

**SIB** [Aside]

To see and the base fellow do not leave's alone too!

**BEAUFORT**
'Tis an excellent habit this. Where were you born, sweet?

**SIB**
I am a Suffolk woman, my lord.

**BEAUFORT**
Believe it, every county you breathe on is the sweeter for you. Let me see your hand.

[Attempting to take her hand from her glove]

The case is loath to part with the jewel! Fairest one, I have skill in palmistry.

**SIB**
Good my lord, what do you find there?

**BEAUFORT**
In good earnest, I do find written here all my good fortune lies in your hand.

**SIB**
You'll keep a very bad house then; you may see by the smallness of the table.

**BEAUFORT**
Who is your sweetheart?

**SIB**
Sweetheart!

**BEAUFORT**
Yes, come, I must sift you to know it.

**SIB**
I am a sieve too coarse for your lordship's manchet.

**BEAUFORT**
Nay, pray you tell me, for I see your husband is an unhandsome fellow.

**SIB**
Oh, my lord, I took him by weight, not fashion. Goldsmiths' wives taught me that way of bargain, and some ladies swerve not to follow the example.

**BEAUFORT**
But will you not tell me who is your private friend?

**SIB**
Yes, and you'll tell me who is yours.

**BEAUFORT**
Shall I show you her?

**SIB**
Yes. When will you?

**BEAUFORT**
Instantly.

[He hands her a mirror.]

Look, there you may see her.

**SIB**
I'll break the glass; 'tis now worth nothing.

**BEAUFORT**
Why?

**SIB**
You have made it a flattering one.

**BEAUFORT**
I have a summer-house for you: a fine place to flatter solitariness. Will you come and lie there?

**SIB**
No, my lord.

**BEAUFORT**
Your husband has promis'd me. Will you not?

**SIB**
I must wink, I tell you, or say nothing.

**BEAUFORT**
So, I'll kiss you and wink too.

[He kisses her.]

Midnight is Cupid's holiday.

[Enter **KNAVESBEE**.

**KNAVESBEE** [Aside]
By this time 'tis concluded.—Will you go, my lord?

**BEAUFORT** [To **SIB**] I leave with you my best wishes till I see you.

**KNAVESBEE**
This now, if I may borrow our lawyer's phrase, is my wife's imparlance; at her next appearance she must answer your declaration.

**BEAUFORT**
You follow it well, sir.

[Exeunt **BEAUFORT** and **KNAVESBEE**.

**SIB**
Did I not know my husband
Of so base, contemptible nature, I should think
'Twere but a trick to try me; but it seems
They are both in wicked earnest, and methinks
Upon the sudden I have a great mind to loathe
This scurvy, unhandsome way my lord has ta'en
To compass me. Why, 'tis for all the world
As if he should come to steal some apricocks
My husband kept for's own tooth, and climb up
Upon his head and shoulders. I'll go to him;
He will put me into brave clothes and rich jewels:
'Twere a very ill part in me not to go,
His mercer and his goldsmith else might curse me.
And what I'll do here, a' my troth yet I know not.
Women, though puzzl'd with these subtle deeds,
May, as i' th' spring, pick physic out of weeds.

[Exit.


SCENE II - Chamlet's Shop


Enter a shop being discover'd. **WATER CHAMLET**, two prentices; **GEORGE** and **RALPH**.

**GEORGE**
What is't you lack, you lack, you lack?
Stuffs for the belly or the back?
Silk grogans, satins, velvet fine,
The rosy-colour'd carnadine,
Your nutmeg hue, or gingerline,
Cloth of tissue, or tabine,
That like beaten gold will shine
In your amorous ladies' eyne,
Whilst you their softer silks do twine:

[Enter **RACHEL**.

What is't you lack, you lack, you lack?

**RACHEL**
I do lack content, sir, content I lack: have you or your worshipful master here any content to sell?

**GEORGE**
If content be a stuff to be sold by the yard, you may have content at home and never go abroad for't.

**RACHEL**
Do, cut me three yards; I'll pay for 'em.

**GEORGE**
There's all we have i' th' shop; we must know what you'll give for 'em first.

**CHAMLET**
Why, Rachel, sweet Rachel, my bosom Rachel,
How didst thou get forth? Thou wert here, sweet Rac,
Within this hour, even in my very heart!

**RACHEL**
Away! Or stay still, I'll away from thee;
One bed shall never hold us both again,
Nor one roof cover us: didst thou bring home—

**GEORGE**
What is't you lack, you lack, you lack?

**RACHEL**
Peace, bandog!
Bandog, give me leave to speak, or I'll—

**GEORGE**
Shall I not follow my trade? I'm bound to't,
And my master bound to bring me up in't.

**CHAMLET**
Peace, good George, give her anger leave;
Thy mistress will be quiet presently.

**RACHEL**
Quiet? I defy thee and quiet too.
Quiet thy bastards thou hast brought home!

**GEORGE AND RALPH**
What is't you lack, you lack? Etc.

**RACHEL**

Death, give me an ell! Has one bawling cur
Rais'd up another? Two dogs upon me!
And the old bearward will not succour me,
I'll stave 'em off myself. Give me an ell, I say!

**GEORGE**
Give her not an inch, master; she'll take two ells if you do.

**CHAMLET**
Peace, George and Ralph; no more words, I charge you.
And Rachel, sweet wife, be more temperate.
I know your tongue speaks not by the rule
And guidance of your heart, when you proclaim
The pretty children of my virtuous
And noble kinswoman, whom in life you knew
Above my praise's reach, to be my bastards.
This is not well, although your anger did it;
Pray, chide your anger for it.

**RACHEL**
Sir, sir, your gloss
Of kinswoman cannot serve turn; 'tis stale
And smells too rank. Though your shop-wares you vent
With your deceiving lights, yet your chamber stuff
Shall not pass so with me, I say, and I will prove—

**GEORGE**
What is't you lack?

[Enter two children; **MARIA** and **EDWARD** Cressingham.

**CHAMLET**
Why, George, I say!

**RACHEL**
Lecher, I say, I'll be divorc'd from thee;
I'll prove 'em thy bastards, and thou insufficient.

[Exit **RACHEL**.

**MARIA**
What said my angry cousin to you, sir?
That we were bastards?

**EDWARD**
I hope she meant not us.

**CHAMLET**

No, no,
My pretty cousin, she meant George and Ralph;
Rage will speak anything, but they are ne'er the worse.

**GEORGE**
Yes, indeed, forsooth, she spoke to us, but chiefly to Ralph, because she knows he has but one stone.

**RALPH**
No more of that if you love me, George; this is not the way to keep a quiet house.

**MARIA**
Truly, sir, I would not, for more treasure
Than ever I saw yet, be in your house
A cause of discord.

**EDWARD**
And do you think I would, sister?

**MARIA**
No, indeed, Ned.

[Enter **FRANKLIN** disguised as a gentleman and young **CRESSINGHAM** disguis'd as his tailor.

**EDWARD**
Why did you not speak for me with you then,
And said we could not have done so?

**CHAMLET**
No more, sweet cousins, now. Speak, George: customers approach.

**CRESSINGHAM** [Aside to **FRANKLIN**]
Is the barber prepar'd?

**FRANKLIN** [Aside to **CRESSINGHAM**]
With ignorance enough to go through with it. So near I am to him, we must call cousins: would thou wert as sure to hit the tailor.

**CRESSINGHAM** [Aside to **FRANKLIN**]
If I do not steal away handsomely, let me never play the tailor again.

**GEORGE**
What is't you lack? Etc.

**FRANKLIN**
Good satins, sir.

**GEORGE**

The best in Europe, sir. Here's a piece worth a piece every yard of him; the King of Naples wears no better silk. Mark his gloss; he dazzles the eye to look upon him.

**FRANKLIN**
Is he not gumm'd?

**GEORGE**
Gumm'd! He has neither mouth nor tooth, how can he be gumm'd?

**FRANKLIN**
Very pretty!

**CHAMLET**
An especial good piece of silk; the worm never spun a finer thread, believe it, sir.

**FRANKLIN** [To **CRESSINGHAM**]
Gascoyn, you have some skill in it.

**CHAMLET**
Your tailor, sir?

**FRANKLIN**
Yes, sir.

**CRESSINGHAM**
A good piece, sir; but let's see more choice.

**RALPH** [Aside to **CRESSINGHAM**]
Tailor, drive through; you know your bribes!

**CRESSINGHAM** [Aside to **RALPH**]
Mum: he bestows forty pounds if I say the word.

**RALPH** [Aside to **CRESSINGHAM**]
Strike through; there's poundage for you then.

**FRANKLIN**
Ay, marry; I like this better. What sayst thou, Gascoyn?

**CRESSINGHAM**
A good piece indeed, sir.

**GEORGE**
The great Turk has worse satin at's elbow than this, sir.

**FRANKLIN**
The price?

**CHAMLET**
Look on the mark, George.

**GEORGE** [Aside to **CHAMLET**]
O, souse and P, by my facks, sir.

**CHAMLET**
The best sort then: sixteen a yard, nothing to be bated.

**FRANKLIN**
Fie, sir, fifteen's too high! Yet so. [To **CRESSINGHAM**] How many yards will service for my suit, sirrah?

**CRESSINGHAM**
Nine yards; you can have no less, Sir Andrew.

**FRANKLIN**
But I can, sir, if you please to steal less; I had but eight in my last suit.

**CRESSINGHAM**
You pinch us too near, in faith, Sir Andrew.

**FRANKLIN**
Yet can you pinch out a false pair of sleeves to a frizado doublet?

**GEORGE**
No, sir, some purses and pin-pillows perhaps; a tailor pays for his kissing that ways.

**FRANKLIN** [To **CHAMLET**] Well, sir, eight yards; eight fifteens I give, and cut it.

**CHAMLET**
I cannot, truly, sir.

**GEORGE**
My master must be no subsidy-man, sir, if he take such fifteens.

**FRANKLIN**
I am at highest, sir, if you can take money.

**CHAMLET**
Well, sir, I'll give you the buying once; I hope to gain it in your custom. Want you nothing else, sir?

**FRANKLIN**
Not at this time, sir.

**CRESSINGHAM**
Indeed, but you do, Sir Andrew. I must needs deliver my lady's message to you; she enjoin'd me by oath to do it: she commanded me to move you for a new gown.

**FRANKLIN**
Sirrah, I'll break your head if you motion it again.

**CRESSINGHAM**
I must endanger myself for my lady, sir; you know she's to go to my Lady Trenchmore's wedding, and to be seen there without a new gown! She'll have ne'er an eye to be seen there, for her fingers in 'em. Nay, by my fack, sir, I do not think she'll go, and then, the cause known, what a discredit 'twill be to you!

**FRANKLIN**
Not a word more, goodman snipsnapper, for your ears! What comes this to, sir?

**CHAMLET**
Six pound, sir.

**FRANKLIN** [Giving him money]
There's your money. [To **CRESSINGHAM**] Will you take this and be gone, and about your business presently?

**CRESSINGHAM**
Troth, sir, I'll see some stuffs for my lady first. I'll tell her at least I did my good will. [To **GEORGE**] A fair piece of cloth of silver, pray you now.

**GEORGE**
Or cloth of gold if you please, sir, as rich as ever the sophy wore.

**FRANKLIN**
You are the arrantest villain of a tailor that ever sat cross-legg'd! What do you think a gown of this stuff will come to?

**CRESSINGHAM**
Why, say it be forty pound, sir: what's that to you? Three thousand a year I hope will maintain it.

**FRANKLIN**
It will, sir; very good. You were best be my overseer! Say I be not furnish'd with money, how then?

**CRESSINGHAM**
A very fine excuse in you! Which place of ten now will you send me for a hundred pound to bring it presently?

**CHAMLET**
Sir, sir, your tailor persuades you well; 'tis for your credit, and the great content of your lady.

**FRANKLIN**
'Tis for your content, sir, and my charges. [To **CRESSINGHAM**] Never think, goodman falsestitch, to come to the mercers with me again. Pray, will you see if my cousin Sweetball the barber, he's nearest hand, be furnish'd, and bring me word instantly.

**CRESSINGHAM**

I fly, sir.

[Exit **CRESSINGHAM**.

**FRANKLIN**
You may fly, sir; you have clipt somebody's wings for it to piece out your own. An arrant thief you are.

**CHAMLET**
Indeed, he speaks honestly and justly, sir.

**FRANKLIN**
You expect some gain, sir: there's your cause of love.

**CHAMLET**
Surely I do a little, sir.

**FRANKLIN**
And what might be the price of this?

**CHAMLET**
This is thirty a yard; but if you'll go to forty, here's a nonpareil.

**FRANKLIN**
So, there's a matter of forty pound for a gown cloth.

**CHAMLET**
Thereabouts, sir. Why, sir, there are far short of your means that wear the like.

**FRANKLIN**
Do you know my means, sir?

**GEORGE**
By overhearing your tailor, sir, three thousand a year; but if you'd have a petticoat for your lady, here's a stuff.

**FRANKLIN**
Are you another tailor, sirrah? Here's a knave! What are you?

**GEORGE**
You are such another gentleman. But for the stuff, sir, 'tis L. s. and d.; for the turn stripp'd a' purpose, a yard and a quarter broad too, which is the just depth of a woman's petticoat.

**FRANKLIN**
And why stripp'd for a petticoat?

**GEORGE**
Because if they abuse their petticoats, there are abuses stripp'd, then 'tis taking them up, and they may be stripp'd and whipp'd too.

**FRANKLIN**
Very ingenious.

**GEORGE**
Then it is likewise stripp'd standing, between which is discover'd the open part, which is now call'd the placket.

**FRANKLIN**
Why, was it ever call'd otherwise?

**GEORGE**
Yes; while the word remain'd pure in his original, the Latin tongue, who have no K's, it was call'd the placet, a placendo, a thing or place to please.

**FRANKLIN**
Better and worse still.

Enter young **CRESSINGHAM**.

Now, sir, you come in haste; what says my cousin?

**CRESSINGHAM**
Protest, sir, he's half angry that either you should think him unfurnish'd, or not furnish'd for your use. There's a hundred pound ready for you; he desires you to pardon his coming: his folks are busy and his wife trimming a gentleman, but at your first approach the money wants but telling.

**FRANKLIN**
He would not trust you with it. I con him thanks for that: he knows what trade you are of. [To **CHAMLET**] Well, sir, pray, cut him patterns; he may in the meantime know my lady's liking. Let your man take the pieces whole with the lowest prices, and walk with me to my cousin's.

**CHAMLET**
With all my heart, sir. Ralph, your cloak, and go with the gentleman; look you give good measure.

**CRESSINGHAM**
Look you, carry a good yard with you.

**RALPH**
The best i' th' shop, sir, yet we have none bad. You'll have the stuff for the petticoat too?

**FRANKLIN**
No, sir, the gown only.

**CRESSINGHAM**
By all means, sir. Not the petticoat? That were holiday upon working-day, i'faith.

**FRANKLIN**

You are so forward for a knave, sir!

**CRESSINGHAM**
'Tis for your credit and my lady's both I do it, sir.

**FRANKLIN** [To **CHAMLET**]
Your man is trusty, sir?

**CHAMLET**
O sir, we keep none but those we dare trust, sir! [Aside to **RALPH**] Ralph, have a care of light gold.

**RALPH** [Aside to **CHAMLET**]
I warrant you, sir, I'll take none.

**FRANKLIN**
Come, sirrah. Fare you well.

**CHAMLET**
Pray, know my shop another time, sir.

**FRANKLIN**
That I shall, sir, from all the shops i' th' town. 'Tis the Lamb in Lombard Street.

[Exeunt **FRANKLIN, CRESSINGHAM, RALPH.**

**GEORGE**
A good morning's work, sir. If this custom would but last long, you might shut up your shop and live privately.

**CHAMLET**
O George, but here's a grief that takes away all the gains and joy of all my thrift!

**GEORGE**
What's that, sir?

**CHAMLET**
Thy mistress, George; her frowardness sours all my comfort.

**GEORGE**
Alas, sir, they are but squibs and crackers; they'll soon die: you know her flashes of old.

**CHAMLET**
But they fly so near me that they burn me, George; they are as ill as muskets charged with bullets.

**GEORGE**
She has discharg'd herself now, sir; you need not fear her.

**CHAMLET**

No man can live without his affliction, George.

**GEORGE**
As you cannot without my mistress.

**CHAMLET**
Right, right, there's harmony in discords: this lamp of love while any oil is left can never be extinct; it may, like a snuff, wink and seem to die, but up he will again and show his head. I cannot be quiet, George, without my wife at home.

**GEORGE**
And when she's at home, you're never quiet, I'm sure; a fine life you have on't. Well, sir, I'll do my best to find her and bring her back if I can.

**CHAMLET**
Do, honest George, at Knavesbee's house, that varlet's—
There's her haunt and harbour—who enforces
A kinsman on her and she calls him cousin.
Restore her, George, to ease this heart that's vex'd;
The best new suit that e'er thou worest is next.

**GEORGE**
I thank you aforehand, sir.

[Exeunt.

SCENE III - Outside Sweetball's House

Enter **FRANKLIN** and young **CRESSINGHAM** disguised as before, **RALPH** carrying the stuffs, **SWEETBALL** the Barber, **BOY**.

**BARBER**
Were it of greater moment than you speak of, noble sir, I hope you think me sufficient, and it shall be effectually performed.

**FRANKLIN**
I could wish your wife did not know it, coz. Women's tongues are not always tuneable; I may many ways requite it.

**BARBER**
Believe me, she shall not, sir, which will be the hardest thing of all.

**FRANKLIN**
Pray you, dispatch him then.

**BARBER**

With the celerity a man tells gold to him.

**FRANKLIN** [Aside]
He hits a good comparison! [To **RALPH**] Give my waste-good your stuffs and go with my cousin, sir; he'll presently dispatch you.

**RALPH**
Yes, sir.

**BARBER**
Come with me, youth; I am ready for you in my more private chamber.

[Exeunt **BARBER** and **RALPH**.

**FRANKLIN**
Sirrah, go you show your lady the stuffs, and let her choose her colour. Away; you know whither. Boy, prithee lend me a brush i' th' meantime. Do you tarry all day now?

**CRESSINGHAM**
That I will, sir, and all night too ere I come again.

[Exit young **CRESSINGHAM** with the stuffs.

**BOY**
Here's a brush, sir.

**FRANKLIN**
A good child!

**BARBER** [within]
What, Toby!

**BOY**
Anon, sir.

**BARBER** within
Why, when, goodman picklock?

**BOY**
I must attend my master, sir. I come!

**FRANKLIN**
Do, pretty lad.

[Exit Boy.

So, take water at Cole Harbour.
An easy mercer and an innocent barber!

[Exit **FRANKLIN** with the brush.

SCENE IV - A Chamber in Sweetball's House

Enter **BARBER, RALPH, BOY**.

**BARBER**
So, friend, I'll now dispatch you presently. Boy, reach me my dismembering instrument and let my cauterizer be ready, and, hark you, snip snap!

**BOY**
Ay, sir.

**BARBER**
See if my lixivium, my fomentation be provided first, and get my rollers, bolsters, and pledgets arm'd.

**RALPH**
Nay, good sir, dispatch my business first; I should not stay from my shop.

**BARBER**
You must have a little patience, sir, when you are a patient; if praeputium be not too much perish'd, you shall lose but little by it, believe my art for that.

**RALPH**
What's that, sir?

**BARBER**
Marry, if there be exulceration between praeputium and glans, by my faith, the whole penis may be endanger'd as far as os pubis.

**RALPH**
What's this you talk on, sir?

**BARBER**
If they be gangren'd once, testiculi, vesica, and all may run to mortification.

**RALPH**
What a pox does this barber talk on?

**BARBER**
O fie, youth, pox is no word of art: morbus Gallicus, or Neopolitamus had been well. Come, friend, you must not be nice; open your griefs freely to me.

**RALPH**
Why, sir, I open my grief to you: I want my money.

**BARBER**

Take you no care for that: your worthy cousin has given me part in hand, and the rest I know he will upon your recovery, and I dare take his word.

**RALPH**

'Sdeath, where's my ware?

**BARBER**

Ware! That was well: the word is cleanly, though not artful. Your ware is that I must see.

**RALPH**

My tabine and cloth of tissue!

**BARBER**

You will neither have tissue nor issue if you linger in your malady; better a member cut off than endanger the whole microcosm.

**RALPH**

Barber, you are not mad?

**BARBER**

I do begin to fear you are subject to subeth, unkindly sleeps, which have bred oppilations in your brain. Take heed, the symptoma will follow, and this may come to frenzy: begin with the first cause, which is the pain of your member.

**RALPH**

Do you see my yard, barber?

**BARBER**

Now you come to the purpose; 'tis that I must see indeed.

**RALPH**

You shall feel it, sir. Death, give me my fifty pounds or my ware again, or I'll measure out your anatomy by the yard!

**BARBER**

Boy, my cauterizing iron red-hot!

[Exit **BOY** then re-enter with iron.

**BOY**

'Tis here, sir.

**BARBER**

If you go further, I take my dismembering knife.

**RALPH**

Where's the knight, your cousin? The thief! And the tailor with my cloth of gold and tissue?

**BOY**
The gentleman that sent away his man with the stuffs is gone a pretty while since; he has carried away our new brush.

**BARBER**
O, that brush hurts my heart's side! Cheated! Cheated! He told me that your virga had a burning-fever.

**RALPH**
A pox on your virga, barber!

**BARBER**
And that you would be bashful and asham'd to show your head.

**RALPH**
I shall so hereafter, but here it is; you see yet my head, my hair, and my wit, and here are my heels that I must show to my master if the cheaters be not found. And barber, provide thee plasters: I will break thy head with every basin under the pole!

[Exit **RALPH**.

**BARBER**
Cool the lixivium and quench the cauterizer;
I am partly out of my wits and partly mad.
My razor's at my heart: these storms will make
My sweetballs stink, my harmless basins shake.

[Exeunt.


ACT III

SCENE I - Lord Beaufort's House

Enter **MISTRESS GEORGE CRESSINGHAM** disguised as Selenger, **SIB**.

**MISTRESS CRESSINGHAM**
You're welcome, mistress, as I may speak it,
But my lord will give it a sweeter emphasis.
I'll give him knowledge of you.

Exiturus.

**SIB**
Good sir, stay.
Methinks it sounds sweetest upon your tongue:

I'll wish you to go no further for my welcome.

**MISTRESS CRESSINGHAM**
Mine! It seems you never heard good music
That commend a bagpipe. Hear his harmony.

**SIB**
Nay, good now, let me borrow of your patience;
I'll pay you again before I rise tomorrow.
If it please you—

**MISTRESS CRESSINGHAM**
What would you, forsooth?

**SIB**
Your company, sir.

**MISTRESS CRESSINGHAM**
My attendance you should have, mistress, but that my lord expects it, and 'tis his due.

**SIB**
And must be paid upon the hour? That's too strict; any time of the day will serve.

**MISTRESS CRESSINGHAM**
Alas, 'tis due every minute, and paid, 'tis due again, or else I forfeit my recognisance, the cloth I wear of his.

**SIB**
Come, come, pay it double at another time, and 'twill be quitted; I have a little use of you.

**MISTRESS CRESSINGHAM**
Of me, forsooth! Small use can be made of me: if you have suit to my lord, none can speak better for you than you may yourself.

**SIB**
Oh, but I am bashful.

**MISTRESS CRESSINGHAM**
So am I, in troth, mistress.

**SIB**
Now I remember me: I have a toy to deliver your lord that's yet unfinish'd, and you may further me. Pray you, your hands, while I unwind this skein of gold from you; 'twill not detain you long.

[She unwinds the skein around her wrists.]

**MISTRESS CRESSINGHAM**
You wind me into your service prettily; with all the haste you can, I beseech you.

**SIB**

If it tangle not, I shall soon have done.

**MISTRESS CRESSINGHAM**

No, it shall not tangle if I can help it, forsooth.

**SIB**

If it do, I can help it. Fear not this thing of long length; you shall see I can bring you to a bottom.

**MISTRESS CRESSINGHAM**

I think so too: if it be not bottomless, this length will reach it.

**SIB**

It becomes you finely, but I forewarn you, and remember it, your enemy gain not this advantage of you: you are his prisoner then, for look you, you are mine now, my captive manacled; I have your hands in bondage.

Grasps the skein between her hands.

**MISTRESS CRESSINGHAM**

'Tis a good lesson, mistress, and I am perfect in it; another time I'll take out this, and learn another. Pray you, release me now.

**SIB**

I could kiss you now, spite of your teeth, if it please me.

**MISTRESS CRESSINGHAM**

But you could not, for I could bite you with the spite of my teeth, if it pleases me.

**SIB**

Well, I'll not tempt you so far; I show it but for rudiment.

**MISTRESS CRESSINGHAM**

When I go a-wooing, I'll think on't again.

**SIB**

In such an hour I learnt it. Say I should,
In recompense of your hands' courtesy,
Make you a fine wrist-favour of this gold,
With all the letters of your name emboss'd
On a soft tress of hair, which I shall cut
From mine own fillet, whose ends should meet and close
In a fast true-love knot: would you wear it
For my sake, sir?

**MISTRESS CRESSINGHAM**

I think not, truly, mistress:

My wrists have enough of this gold already;
Would they were rid on't. Yet, pray you, have done;
In troth, I'm weary.

**SIB**
And what a virtue
Is here express'd in you, which had lain hid
But for this trial. Weary of gold, sir?
Oh, that the close engrossers of this treasure
Could be so free to put it off of hand,
What a new-mended world would here be!
It shows a generous condition in you;
In sooth, I think I shall love you dearly for't.

**MISTRESS CRESSINGHAM**
But if they were in prison, as I am,
They would be glad to buy their freedom with it.

**SIB**
Surely no: there are that, rather than release
This dear companion, do lie in prison with it;
Yes, and will die in prison too.

**MISTRESS CRESSINGHAM**
'Twere pity but the hangman did enfranchise both.

[Enter **BEAUFORT**.

**BEAUFORT**
Selenger, where are you?

**MISTRESS CRESSINGHAM**
E'en here, my lord. Mistress, pray you, my liberty; you hinder my duty to my lord.

[**BEAUFORT** puts off his hat.

**BEAUFORT**
Nay, sir, one courtesy shall serve us both at this time. You're busy, I perceive; when your leisure next serves you, I would employ you.

**MISTRESS CRESSINGHAM**
You must pardon me, my lord; you see I am entangled here. Mistress, I protest I'll break prison if you free me not; take you no notice?

**SIB**
Oh, cry your honour mercy! You are now at liberty, sir.

[She takes the skein off her wrists.]

**MISTRESS CRESSINGHAM** [Aside]
And I'm glad on't; I'll ne'er give both my hands at once again to a woman's command; I'll put one finger in a hole rather.

**BEAUFORT**
Leave us.

**MISTRESS CRESSINGHAM**
Free leave have you, my lord. [Aside] So I think you may have: filthy beauty, what a white witch thou art!

[Exit **MISTRESS CRESSINGHAM**.

**BEAUFORT**
Lady, y'are welcome.

**SIB**
I did believe it from your page, my lord.

**BEAUFORT**
Your husband sent you to me.

**SIB**
He did, my lord,
With duty and commends unto your honour,
Beseeching you to use me very kindly,
By the same token your lordship gave him grant
Of a new lease of threescore pound a year,
Which he and his should forty years enjoy.

**BEAUFORT**
The token's true, and for your sake, lady
'Tis likely to be better'd, not alone the lease,
But the fee-simple may be his and yours.

**SIB**
I have a suit unto your lordship too
Only myself concerns.

**BEAUFORT**
'Twill be granted, sure,
Tho' it out-value thy husband's.

**SIB**
Nay, 'tis small charge:
Only your good will and good word, my lord.

**BEAUFORT**

The first is thine confirm'd; the second then
Cannot stay long behind.

**SIB**
I love your page, sir.

**BEAUFORT**
Love him! For what?

**SIB**
Oh, the great wisdoms that
Our grandsires had! Do you ask me reason for't?
I love him because I like him, sir.

**BEAUFORT**
My page!

**SIB**
In mine eye he's a most delicate youth,
But in my heart a thing that it would bleed for.

**BEAUFORT**
Either your eye is blinded or your remembrance broken:
Call to mind wherefore you came hither, lady.

**SIB**
I do, my lord: for love, and I am in profoundly.

**BEAUFORT**
You trifle, sure. Do you long for unripe fruit?
'Twill breed diseases in you.

**SIB**
Nothing but worms
In my belly, and there's a seed to expel them;
In mellow, falling fruit I find no relish.

**BEAUFORT**
'Tis true, the youngest vines yield the most clusters,
But the old ever the sweetest grapes.

**SIB**
I can taste of both, sir,
But with the old I am the soonest cloy'd:
The green keep still an edge on appetite.

**BEAUFORT**
Sure you are a common creature.

**SIB**

Did you doubt it?
Wherefore came I hither else? Did you think
That honesty only had been immur'd for you,
And I should bring it as an offertory
Unto your shrine of lust? As it was, my lord,
'Twas meant to you, had not the slippery wheel
Of fancy turn'd when I beheld your page.
Nay, had I seen another before him
In mine eyes better graced, he had been forestall'd.
But as it is—all my strength cannot help—
Beseech you, your good will and good word, my lord;
You may command him, sir, if not affection,
Yet his body, and I desire but that; do't
And I'll command myself your prostitute.

**BEAUFORT**

Y'are a base strumpet! I succeed my page?

**SIB**

Oh, that's no wonder, my lord; the servant oft
Tastes to his master of the daintiest dish
He brings to him. Beseech you, my lord.

**BEAUFORT**

Y'are a bold mischief. And to make me your spokesman,
Your procurer to my servant!

**SIB**

Do you shrink at that?
Why, you have done worse without the sense of ill
With a full free conscience of a libertine.
Judge your own sin:
Was it not worse with a damn'd broking-fee
To corrupt a husband, state him a pander
To his own wife, by virtue of a lease
Made to him and your bastard issue, could you get 'em?
What a degree of baseness call you this?
'Tis a poor sheep-stealer provok'd by want
Compar'd unto a capital traitor; the master
To his servant may be recompens'd, but the husband
To his wife never.

**BEAUFORT**

Your husband shall smart for this!

[Exit **BEAUFORT**.

**SIB**

Hang him, do; you have brought him to deserve it:
Bring him to the punishment; there I'll join with you.
I loathe him to the gallows! Hang your page too;
One mourning gown shall serve for both of them.
This trick hath kept mine honesty secure;
Best soldiers use policy: the lion's skin
Becomes not the body when 'tis too great,
But then the fox's may sit close and neat.

[Exit.


SCENE II - A Street Outside a Tavern

Enter **FLESHHOOK, COUNTERBUFF,** and **SWEETBALL** the Barber.

**BARBER**

Now, Fleshhook, use thy talon, set upon his right shoulder; thy sergeant Counterbuff at the left, grasp in his jugulars; and then let me alone to tickle his diaphragma.

**FLESHHOOK**

You are sure he has no protection, sir?

**BARBER**

A protection to cheat and cozen! There was never any granted to that purpose.

**FLESHHOOK**

I grant you that too, sir, but that use has been made of 'em.

**COUNTERBUFF**

Marry, has there, sir. How could else so many broken bankrupts play up and down by their creditors' noses, and we dare not touch 'em?

**BARBER**

That's another case, Counterbuff; there's privilege to cozen: but here cozenage went before, and there's no privilege for that. To him boldly! I will spend all the scissors in my shop, but I'll have him snapp'd.

**COUNTERBUFF**

Well, sir, if he come within the length of large mace once, we'll teach him to cozen.

**BARBER**

Marry, hang him, teach him no more cozenage; he's too perfect in't already. Go gingerly about it, lay your mace on gingerly, and spice him soundly.

**COUNTERBUFF**

He's at the tavern, you say?

**BARBER**
At the Man in the Moon, above stairs. So soon as he comes down, and the bush left at his back, Ralph is the dog behind him: he watches to give us notice; be ready then, my dear bloodhounds. You shall deliver him to Newgate, from thence to the hangman; his body I will beg of the sheriffs, for at the next lecture I am likely to be the master of my anatomy. Then will I vex every vein about him; I will find where his disease of cozenage lay, whether in the vertebrae, or in os coxendix: but I guess I shall find it descend from humore, through the thorax, and lie just at his fingers' ends.

[Enter **RALPH**.

**RALPH**
Be in readiness, for he's coming this way, alone too. Stand to't like gentleman and yeoman: so soon as he is in sight, I'll go fetch my master.

**BARBER**
I have had a conquassation in my cerebrum ever since the disaster, and now it takes me again: if it turn to a megrim, I shall hardly abide the sight of him.

**RALPH**
My action of defamation shall be clapp'd on him too; I will make him appear to't in the shape of a white sheet all embroidered over with peccavis.

[Enter **FRANKLIN**.

Look about; I'll go fetch my master.

[Exit **RALPH**.

**COUNTERBUFF**
I arrest you, sir.

[**COUNTERBUFF** and **FLESHHOOK** grab **FRANKLIN**.

**FRANKLIN**
Ha! Qui va là? Que pensez-vous faire, messieurs? Me voulez-vous dérober? Je n'ai point d'argent: je suis un pauvre gentilhomme français.

**BARBER**
Whoop! Pray you, sir, speak English. You did when you bought cloth of gold at six nihils a yard, when Ralph's praeputium was exulcerated.

**FRANKLIN**
Que voulez-vous? Me voulez-vous tuer? Les Français ne sont point ennemis.

[Giving them his purse]

Voilà ma bourse; que voulez-vous d'avantage?

**COUNTERBUFF**
Is not your name Franklin, sir?

**FRANKLIN**
Je n'ai point de joyaux que cestui-ci, et c'est à monsieur l'ambassadeur. Il m'envoie à ses affaires, et vous empêchez mon service.

**COUNTERBUFF**
Sir, we are mistaken, for aught I perceive.

[Enter **CHAMLET** and **RALPH** hastily.

**CHAMLET**
So, so, you have caught him; that's well. How do you, sir?

**FRANKLIN**
Vous semblez être un homme courtois; je vous prie entendez mes affaires: il y a ici deux ou trois canailles qui m'ont assiégé, un pauvre étranger qui ne leur ai fait nul mal, ni donné mauvaise parole, ni tiré mon épée. L'un me prend par une épaule, et me frappe deux livre pesant; l'autre me tire par le bras, il parle je ne sais quoi. Je leur ai donné ma bourse, et s'ils ne me veulent point laisser aller; que ferai-je monsieur?

**CHAMLET**
This is a Frenchman it seems, sirs.

**COUNTERBUFF**
We can find no other in him, sir, and what that is we know not.

**CHAMLET**
He's very like the man we seek for, else my lights go false.

**BARBER**
In your shop they may, sir, but here they go true: this is he.

**RALPH**
The very same, sir, as sure as I am Ralph: this is the rascal.

**COUNTERBUFF**
Sir, unless you will absolutely challenge him the man, we dare not proceed further.

**FLESHHOOK**
I fear we are too far already.

**CHAMLET**
I know not what to say to't.

[Enter **MARGARITA**, a French bawd.

**MARGARITA**
Bon jour, bon jour, gentilhommes.

**BARBER**
How now! More news from France?

**FRANKLIN**
Cette femme ici est de mon pays. Madame, je vous prie leur dire mon pays; il m'ont retardé, je ne sais pourquoi.

**MARGARITA**
Etes-vous de France, monsieur?

**FRANKLIN**
Madame, vrai est que je les ai trompés, et suis arrête, et n'ai nul moyen d'échapper qu'en changeant mon langage. Aidez-moi en cette affaire. Je vous connois bien, où vous tenez un bordeau; vous et les votres en serez de mieux.

**MARGARITA**
Laissez faire à moi. Etes-vous de Lyons, dites-vous?

**FRANKLIN**
De Lyons, ma chère dame.

[Embrace and complement.

**MARGARITA**
Mon cousin! Je suis bien aise de vous voir en bonne disposition.

**FRANKLIN**
Ma cousine!

**CHAMLET**
This is a Frenchman, sure.

**BARBER**
If he be, 'tis the likest an Englishman that ever I saw; all his dimensions, proportions! Had I but the dissecting of his heart, in capsula cordis could I find it now, for a Frenchman's heart is more quassative and subject to tremor than an Englishman's.

**CHAMLET**
Stay, we'll further enquire of this gentlewoman. Mistress, if you have so much English to help us with, as I think you have, for I have long seen you about London, pray, tell us, and truly tell us, is this gentleman a natural Frenchman or no?

**MARGARITA**

Ey, begar, de Frenchman, born à Lyons, my cozin.

**CHAMLET**
Your cousin? If he be not your cousin, he's my cousin, sure!

**MARGARITA**
Ey conosh his père, what you call his fadre? He sell poissons.

**BARBER**
Sell poisons? His father was a 'pothecary then.

**MARGARITA**
No, no, poissons, what you call fish, fish.

**BARBER**
Oh, he was a fishmonger.

**MARGARITA**
Oui, oui.

**CHAMLET**
Well, well, we are mistaken, I see; pray you, so tell him, and request him not to be offended. An honest man may look like a knave, and be ne'er the worse for't. The error was in our eyes, and now we find it in his tongue.

**MARGARITA**
J'essayerai encore une fois, monsieur cousin, pour votre sauveté. Allez-vous en; votre liberté est suffisante. Je gagnerai le reste pour mon devoir, et vous aurez votre part à mon école. J'ai une fille qui parle un peu Français; elle conversera avec vous à la Fleur-de-Lis en Turnbull Street. Mon cousin, ayez soin de vous-même, et trompez ces ignorans.

**FRANKLIN**
Cousine, pour l'amour de vous, et principalement pour moi, je suis content de m'en aller. Je trouverai votre école, et si vos écoliers me sont agréables, je tirerai à l'épée seule, et si d'aventure je la rompe, je payerai dix sous. Et pour ce vieux fol, et ces deux canailles, ce poulain Snipsnap, et l'autre bonnet rond, je les verrai pendre premier que je les vois.

**CHAMLET**
So, so, she has got him off; but I perceive much anger in his countenance still. And what says he, madam?

**MARGARITA**
Moosh, moosh anger, but ey conosh heer lodging shall cool him very well. Dere is a kinswomans can moosh allay heer heat and heer spleen; she shall do for my saka, and he no trobla you.

**CHAMLET** [Giving her money]
Look, there is earnest, but thy reward's behind. Come to my shop, the Holy Lamb in Lombard Street; thou hast one friend more than e'er thou hadst.

**MARGARITA**

Tank u, monsieur; shall visit u. Ey make all pacifie; à votre service très humblement, tree, four, five fool of u.

[Exit **MARGARITA**.

**CHAMLET**

What's to be done now?

**COUNTERBUFF**

To pay us for our pains, sir, and better reward us, that we may be provided against further danger that may come upon's for false imprisonment.

**CHAMLET**

All goes false, I think. What do you, neighbour Sweetball?

**BARBER**

I must phlebotomise, sir, but my almanac says the sign is in Taurus. I dare not cut my own throat, but if I find any precedent that ever barber hang'd himself, I'll be the second example.

**RALPH**

This was your ill lixivium, barber, to cause all to be cheated.

**COUNTERBUFF**

What say you to us, sir?

**CHAMLET**

Good friends, come to me at a calmer hour;
My sorrows lie in heaps upon me now.
What you have, keep; if further trouble follow,
I'll take it on me: I would be press'd to death.

**COUNTERBUFF**

Well, sir, for this time we'll leave you.

**BARBER**

I will go with you, officers; I will walk with you in the open street though it be a scandal to me, for now I have no care of my credit. A cacokenny is run all over me.

[Exeunt **BARBER, FLESHHOOK, COUNTERBUFF**]. Enter **GEORGE**.

**CHAMLET**

What shall we do now, Ralph?

**RALPH**

Faith, I know not, sir. Here comes George; it may be he can tell you.

**CHAMLET**
And there I look for more disaster still;
Yet George appears in a smiling countenance.
Ralph, home to the shop; leave George and I together.

**RALPH**
I am gone, sir.

[Exit **RALPH**.

**CHAMLET**
Now, George, what better news eastward? All goes ill the tother way.

**GEORGE**
I bring you the best news that ever came about your ears in your life, sir.

**CHAMLET**
Thou putst me in good comfort, George.

**GEORGE**
My mistress, you wife, will never trouble you more.

**CHAMLET**
Ha? Never trouble me more? Of this, George, may be made a sad construction; that phrase we
sometimes use when death makes the separation. I hope it is not so with her, George?

**GEORGE**
No, sir, but she vows she'll never come home again to you, so you shall live quietly, and this I took to be
very good news, sir.

**CHAMLET**
The worst that could be, this candied poison.
I love her, George, and I am bound to do so.
The tongue's bitterness must not separate
United souls: 'twere base and cowardly
For all to yield to the small tongue's assault;
The whole building must not be taken down
For the repairing of a broken window.

**GEORGE**
Ay, but this is a principal, sir. The truth is, she will be divorc'd, she says, and is labouring with her cousin
Knave—What do you call him? I have forgotten the latter end of his name.

**CHAMLET**
Knavesbee, George.

**GEORGE**
Ay, Knave or Knavesbee; one I took it to be.

**CHAMLET**

Why, neither rage nor envy can make a cause, George.

**GEORGE**

Yes, sir, not only at your person, but she shoots at your shop too; she says you vent ware that is not warrantable, braided ware, and that you give not London measure. Women, you know, look for more than a bare yard. And then you keep children in the name of your own, which she suspects came not in at the right door.

**CHAMLET**

She may as well suspect immaculate truth
To be cursed falsehood.

**GEORGE**

Ay, but if she will, she will: she's a woman, sir.

**CHAMLET**

'Tis most true, George. Well, that shall be redress'd:
My cousin Cressingham must yield me pardon;
The children shall home again, and thou shalt conduct 'em, George.

**GEORGE**

That done, I'll be bold to venter once more for her recovery, since you cannot live at liberty; but because you are a rich citizen, you will have your chain about your neck. I think I have a device will bring you together by th' ears again, and then look to 'em as well as you can.

**CHAMLET**

Oh George, amongst all my heavy troubles, this
Is the groaning weight! But restore my wife.

**GEORGE**

Although you ne'er lead hour of quiet life?

**CHAMLET**

I will endeavour 't, George. I'll lend her will
A power and rule to keep all hush'd and still.
Eat we all sweetmeats, we are soonest rotten.

**GEORGE**

A sentence! Pity 't should have been forgotten.

[Exeunt.


ACT IV

Enter **SIR FRANCIS CRESSINGHAM** and a **SURVEYOR** at different doors.

**SURVEYOR**
Where's master steward?

**SIR FRANCIS**
Within. What are you, sir?

**SURVEYOR**
A surveyor, sir.

**SIR FRANCIS**
And an almanac-maker, I take it. Can you tell me what foul weather is toward?

**SURVEYOR**
Marry, the foulest weather is, that your land is flying away.

[Exit **SURVEYOR**.

**SIR FRANCIS**
A most terrible prognostication! All the resort, all the business to my house is to my lady and master steward, whilst Sir Francis stands for a cipher. I have made away myself and my power as if I had done it by deed of gift. Here comes the comptroller of the game.

[Enter **SAUNDER**.

**SAUNDER**
What, are you yet resolved to translate this unnecessary land into ready money?

**SIR FRANCIS**
Translate it?

**SAUNDER**
The conveyances are drawn and the money ready. My lady sent me to you to know directly if you meant to go through in the sale; if not, she resolves of another course.

**SIR FRANCIS**
Thou speakest this cheerfully, methinks, whereas faithful servants were wont to mourn when they beheld the lord that fed and cherish'd them, as by curst enchantments remov'd into another blood. Cressingham of Cressingham has continued for many years, and must the name sink now?

**SAUNDER**
All this is nothing to my lady's resolution; it must be done or she'll not stay in England. She would know whether your son be sent for that must likewise set his hand to th' sale; for otherwise the lawyers say there cannot be a sure conveyance made to the buyer.

**SIR FRANCIS**
Yes, I have sent for him; but I pray thee, think what a hard task 'twill be for a father to persuade his son and heir to make away his inheritance.

**SAUNDER**
Nay, for that use your own logic: I have heard you talk at the sessions terribly against deer-stealers, and that kept you from being put out of the commission.

[Exit **SAUNDER**. Enter young **CRESSINGHAM**.

**SIR FRANCIS**
I do live to see two miseries, one to be commanded by my wife, the other to be censured by my slave.

**CRESSINGHAM** [Kneeling]
That which I have wanted long, and has been cause of my irregular courses, I beseech you let raise me from the ground.

**SIR FRANCIS** [Raising him and giving him money]
Rise, George: there's a hundred pounds for you, and my blessing; with these, your mother's favour. But I hear your studies are become too licentious of late.

**CRESSINGHAM** [Aside]
H'as heard of my cozenage.

**SIR FRANCIS**
What's that you're writing?

**CRESSINGHAM**
Sir, not anything.

**SIR FRANCIS**
Come, I hear there's something coming forth of yours will be your undoing.

**CRESSINGHAM**
Of mine?

**SIR FRANCIS**
Yes, of your writing; somewhat you should write will be dangerous to you. I have a suit to you.

**CRESSINGHAM**
Sir, my obedience makes you commander in all things.

**SIR FRANCIS**
I pray, suppose I had committed some fault,
For which my life and sole estate were forfeit
To the law, and that some great man near the king
Should labour to get my pardon, on condition
He might enjoy my lordship: could you prize

Your father's life above the grievous loss
Of your inheritance?

**CRESSINGHAM**
Yes, and my own life
At stake too.

**SIR FRANCIS**
You promise fair; I come now
To make trial of it. You know I have married
One whom I hold so dear that my whole life
Is nothing but a mere estate depending
Upon her will and her affections to me.
She deserves so well, I cannot longer merit
Than durante beneplacito: 'tis her pleasure,
And her wisdom moves in't too, of which I'll give you
Ample satisfaction hereafter, that I sell
The land my father left me. You change colour!
I have promis'd her to do't, and should I fail,
I must expect the remainder of my life
As full of trouble and vexation
As the suit for a divorce; it lies in you
By setting of your hand unto the sale
To add length to his life that gave you yours.

**CRESSINGHAM**
Sir, I do now ingeniously perceive
Why you said lately somewhat I should write
Would be my undoing, meaning, as I take it,
Setting my hand to this assurance. Oh, good sir,
Shall I pass away my birthright? Oh, remember
There is a malediction denounc'd against it
In holy writ! Will you, for her pleasure,
The inheritance of desolation leave
To your posterity? Think how compassionate
The creatures of the field, that only live
On the wild benefits of nature, are
Unto their young ones; think likewise you may
Have more children by this woman, and by this act
You undo them too. 'Tis a strange precedent this,
To see an obedient son labouring good counsel
To the father! But know, sir, that the spirits
Of my great-grandfather and your father move
At this present in me, and what they bequeath'd you
On their deathbed they charge you not to give away
In the dalliance of a woman's bed. Good sir,
Let it not be thought presumption in me
That I have continued my speech unto this length:

The cause, sir, is urgent and, believe it, you
Shall find her beauty as malevolent unto you
As a red morning that doth still foretell
A foul day to follow. Oh, sir, keep your land!
Keep that to keep your name immortal, and you shall see
All that her malice and proud will procures,
Shall show her ugly heart, but hurt not yours.

**SIR FRANCIS**
Oh, I am distracted, and my very soul
Sends blushes into my cheeks.

[Enter **GEORGE** with the two children; **MARIA** and **EDWARD**.

**CRESSINGHAM**
See here an object
To beget more compassion.

**GEORGE**
O Sir Francis, we have a most lamentable house at home! Nothing to be heard in't but separation and divorces, and such a noise of the spiritual court as if it were a tenement upon London Bridge and built upon the arches.

**SIR FRANCIS**
What's the matter?

**GEORGE**
All about boarding your children: my mistress is departed.

**SIR FRANCIS**
Dead?

**GEORGE**
In a sort she is, and laid out too, for she is run away from my master.

**SIR FRANCIS**
Whither?

**GEORGE**
Seven miles off, into Essex: she vow'd never to leave Barking while she liv'd till these were brought home again.

**SIR FRANCIS**
Oh, they shall not offend her. I am sorry for't.

**MARIA**
I am glad we are come home, sir, for we liv'd in the unquietest house!

**EDWARD**
The angry woman methought grutch'd us our victuals: our new mother is a good soul, and loves us, and does not frown so like a vixen as she does.

**MARIA**
I am at home now, and in heaven methinks: what a comfort 'tis to be under your wing!

**EDWARD**
Indeed, my mother was wont to call me your nestle-cock, and I love you as well as she did.

**SIR FRANCIS**
You are my pretty souls.

**CRESSINGHAM**
Does not the prattle of these move you?

[Enter **SAUNDER, KNAVESBEE,** and **SURVEYOR**.

**SAUNDER**
Look you, sir, here's the conveyance and my lady's solicitor: pray, resolve what to do; my lady is coming down. How now, George? How does thy mistress that sits in a wainscot gown, like a citizen's lure to draw in customers? Oh, she's a pretty mousetrap!

**GEORGE**
She's ill-baited though to take a Welshman; she cannot away with cheese.

**SIR FRANCIS**
And what must I do now?

**KNAVESBEE**
Acknowledge a fine and recovery of the land; then for possession the course is common.

**SIR FRANCIS**
Carry back the writings, sir; my mind in chang'd.

**SAUNDER**
Chang'd! Do not you mean to seal?

[Enter **LADY CRESSINGHAM**.

**SIR FRANCIS**
No, sir, the tide's turn'd.

**SAUNDER** [Aside]
You must temper him like wax or he'll not seal.

**LADY CRESSINGHAM**
Are you come back again? How now, have you done?

**MARIA**
How do you, lady mother?

**LADY CRESSINGHAM**
You are good children. Bid my woman give them some sweetmeats.

**MARIA**
Indeed, I thank you. Is not this a kind mother?

**CRESSINGHAM**
Poor fools, you know not how dear you shall pay for this sugar.

[Exeunt **GEORGE, MARIA, EDWARD**.

**LADY CRESSINGHAM**
What, ha'n't you dispatch'd?

**SIR FRANCIS**
No, sweetest, I am dissuaded by my son
From the sale o' th' land.

**LADY CRESSINGHAM**
Dissuaded by your son!

**SIR FRANCIS**
I cannot get his hand to't.

**LADY CRESSINGHAM**
Where's our steward?
Cause presently that all my beds and hangings
Be taken down; provide carts, pack them up:
I'll to my house i' th' country. Have I studied
The way to your preferment and your children's,
And do you cool i' th' upshot?

**CRESSINGHAM**
With your pardon,
I cannot understand this course a way
To any preferment, rather a direct path
To our ruin.

**LADY CRESSINGHAM**
Oh sir, you are young-sighted!
Show them the project of the land I mean
To buy in Ireland, that shall outvalue yours
Three thousand in a year.

[**KNAVESBEE** shows them a map.

**KNAVESBEE**
Look you, sir: here is Clangibbon, a fruitful country, and well-wooded.

**SIR FRANCIS**
What's this? Marsh-ground?

**KNAVESBEE**
No, these are bogs, but a little cost will drain them. This upper part that runs by the black water is the Cussacks' land, a spacious country, and yields excellent profit by the salmon and fishing for herring. Here runs the Kernesdale, admirable feed for cattle, and hereabout is St. Patrick's Purgatory.

**CRESSINGHAM**
Purgatory! Shall we purchase that too?

**LADY CRESSINGHAM**
Come, come, will you dispatch th' other business?
We may go through with this?

**SIR FRANCIS**
My son's unwilling.

**LADY CRESSINGHAM**
Upon my soul, sir, I'll never bed with you
Till you have seal'd.

**SIR FRANCIS**
Thou hear'st her: on thy blessing
Follow me to th' court and seal.

**CRESSINGHAM**
Sir, were it my death,
Wer't to th' loss of my estate, I vow
To obey you in all things; yet with it remember
There are two young ones living that may curse you.
I pray, dispose part of the money on their
Generous educations.

**LADY CRESSINGHAM**
Fear not you, sir.
The carouche there! When you have dispatch'd
You shall find me at the scrivener's, where I shall
Receive the money.

**CRESSINGHAM**
She'll devour that mass too.

**LADY CRESSINGHAM**
How likest thou my power over him?

**SAUNDER**
Excellent.

**LADY CRESSINGHAM**
This is the height of a great lady's sway,
When her night-service makes her rule i' th' day.

[Exeunt.


SCENE II - Before Knavesbee's House

Enter **KNAVESBEE**.

**KNAVESBEE**
Not yet, Sib? My lord keeps thee so long, th'art welcome, I see, then. And pays sweetly too: a good wench, Sib, th'art, to obey thy husband.

[Enter **SIB**.]

She's come: a hundred mark a year, how fine and easy it comes into mine arms now! Welcome home; what says my lord, Sib?

**SIB**
My lord says you are a cuckold.

**KNAVESBEE**
Ha, ha, ha, ha, I thank him for that bob, i'faith! I'll afford it him again at the same price a month hence, and let the commodity grow as scarce as it will. Cuckold, says his lordship! Ha, ha, I shall burst my sides with laughing, that's the worst! Name not a hundred a year, for then I burst! It smarts not so much as a fillip on the forehead by five parts: what has his dalliance taken from thy lips? 'Tis as sweet as e'er 'twas; let me try else: buss me, sugar-candy.

**SIB**
Forbear; you presume to a lord's pleasure!

**KNAVESBEE**
How's that? Not I, Sib.

**SIB**
Never touch me more;
I'll keep the noble stamp upon my lip,
No under baseness shall deface it now.
You taught me the way; now I am in, I'll keep it.

I have kiss'd ambition, and I love it;
I loathe the memory of every touch
My lip hath tasted from thee!

**KNAVESBEE**
Nay, but sweet Sib,
You do forget yourself.

**SIB**
I will forget
All that I ever was, and nourish new thoughts:
Sirrah, I am a lady.

**KNAVESBEE**
Lord bless us, madam!

**SIB**
I have enjoy'd a lord, that's real possession,
And daily shall, the which all ladies have
Not with their lords.

**KNAVESBEE**
But with your patience, madam,
Who was it that prefer'd you to this ladyship?

**SIB**
'Tis all I am beholding to thee for:
Th'ast brought me out of ignorance into light.
Simple as I was, I thought thee a man
Till I found the difference by a man: thou art
A beast, a horned beast, an ox!

**KNAVESBEE**
Are these
Ladies' terms?

**SIB**
For thy pander's fee,
It shall be laid under the candlestick;
Look for't, I'll leave it for thee.

**KNAVESBEE**
A little lower,
Good your ladyship: my cousin Chamlet
Is in the house; let these things go no further.

**SIB**
'Tis for mine own credit if I forebear,

Not thine, thou bugle-brow'd beast, thou!

[Enter **GEORGE** with rolls of paper.

**GEORGE**
Bidden, bidden, bidden, bidden! So, all these are past; but here's as large a walk to come. If I do not get it up at the feast, I shall be leaner for bidding the guests, I'm sure.

**KNAVESBEE**
How now! Who's this?

**GEORGE** [Reading]
"Doctor Glister et—" What word's this? Fuxor? Oh, uxor! "The doctor and his wife. Master Body et uxor of Bow Lane. Master Knavesbee et uxor."

**KNAVESBEE**
Ha, we are in, whatsoever the matter is.

**GEORGE**
Here's forty couple more in this quarter, but there, the provision bringing in, that puzzles me most. One ox: that will hardly serve for beef too. Five muttons, ten lambs: poor innocents, they'll be devoured too. Three gross of capons—

**KNAVESBEE**
Mercy upon us! What a slaughterhouse is here!

**GEORGE**
Two bushels of small birds, plovers, snipes, woodcocks, partridge, larks. Then for bak'd meats—

**KNAVESBEE**
George, George, what feast is this? 'Tis not for St. George's Day?

**GEORGE**
Cry you mercy, sir, you and your wife are in my roll: my master invites you his guests tomorrow dinner.

**KNAVESBEE**
Dinner say'st thou? He means to feast a month sure.

**GEORGE**
Nay, sir, you make up but a hundred couple.

**KNAVESBEE**
Why, what ship has brought an India home to him that he's so bountiful? Or what friend dead, unknown to us, has so much left to him of arable land, that he means to turn to pasture thus?

**GEORGE**
Nay, 'tis a vessel, sir; a good estate comes all in one bottom to him, and 'tis a question whether ever he find the bottom or no: a thousand a year, that's the uppermost.

**KNAVESBEE**
A thousand a year!

**GEORGE**
To go no further about the bush, sir, now the bird is caught: my master is tomorrow to be married, and amongst the rest invites you a guest at his wedding dinner the second.

**KNAVESBEE**
Married!

**GEORGE**
There is no other remedy for flesh and blood: that will have leave to play whether we will or no, or wander into forbidden pastures.

**KNAVESBEE**
Married! Why, he is married, man! His wife is in my house now; thy mistress is alive, George!

**GEORGE**
That she was, it may be, sir, but dead to him. She play'd a little too rough with him, and he has discarded her; he's divorc'd, sir.

**KNAVESBEE**
He divorc'd! Then is her labour sav'd, for she was labouring a divorce from him.

**GEORGE**
They are well parted then, sir.

**KNAVESBEE**
But wilt thou not speak with her? I'faith, invite her to't.

**GEORGE**
'Tis not my commission, I dare not. Fare you well, sir; I have much business in hand, and the time is short.

**KNAVESBEE**
Nay, but George, I prithee stay. May I report this to her for a certain truth?

**GEORGE**
Wherefore am I employ'd in this invitation, sir?

**KNAVESBEE**
Prithee what is she, his second choice?

**GEORGE**
Truly a goodly presence, likely to bear great children, and great store; she never saw five-and-thirty summers together in her life by her appearance, and comes in her French hood. By my fecks, a great

match 'tis like to be; I am sorry for my old mistress but cannot help it. Pray you, excuse me now, sir, for all the business goes through my hands, none employ'd but myself.

[Exit **GEORGE**.

**KNAVESBEE**
Why, here is news that no man will believe but he that sees.

**SIB**
This and your cuckoldry will be digestion throughout the city dinners and suppers for a month together, there will need no cheese.

**KNAVESBEE**
No more of that, Sib. I'll call my cousin Chamlet and make her partaker of this sport.

[Enter **RACHEL**.

She's come already. Cousin, take't at once, y'are a free woman; your late husband's to be married tomorrow.

**RACHEL**
Married! To whom?

**KNAVESBEE**
To a French hood, byrlakins, as I understand; great cheer prepar'd, and great guests invited, so far I know.

**RACHEL**
What a curst wretch was I to pare my nails today, a Friday too! I look'd for some mischief.

**KNAVESBEE**
Why, I did think this had accorded with your best liking; you sought for him what he has sought for you: a separation, and by divorce too.

**RACHEL**
I'll divorce 'em! Is he to be married to a French hood? I'll dress it the English fashion; ne'er a coach to be had with six horses to strike fire i' th' streets as we go?

**KNAVESBEE**
Will you go home then?

**RACHEL**
Good cousin, help me to whet one of my knives while I sharp the tother; give me a sour apple to set my teeth on edge. I would give five pound for the paring of my nails again! Have you e'er a bird-spit i' th' house? I'll dress one dish to the wedding.

**KNAVESBEE**
This violence hurts yourself the most.

**RACHEL**
I care not who I hurt. Oh my heart, how it beats a' both sides! Will you run with me for a wager into Lombard Street now?

**KNAVESBEE**
I'll walk with you, cousin, a sufficient pace; Sib shall come softly after. I'll bring you through Bearbinder Lane.

**RACHEL**
Bearbinder Lane cannot hold me; I'll the nearest way over St. Mildred's church. If I meet any French hoods by the way, I'll make black patches enow for the rheum.

[Exeunt **KNAVESBEE** and **RACHEL**.

**SIB**
So, 'tis to my wish. Master Knavesbee,
Help to make peace abroad; here you'll find wars:
I'll have a divorce too, with locks and bars.

[Exit.


SCENE III - Chamlet's Shop

Enter **GEORGE, MARGARITA**.

**GEORGE**
Madam, but stay here a little, my master comes instantly. I heard him say he did owe you a good turn, and now's the time to take it. I'll warrant you a sound reward e'er you go.

[Enter **CHAMLET**.

**MARGARITA**
Ey tank u de bon coure, monsieur.

**GEORGE**
Look, he's here already. [Aside] Now would a skillful navigator take in his sails, for sure there is a storm towards.

[Exit **GEORGE**.

**CHAMLET**
Oh, madam, I perceive in your countenance I am beholding to you. All is peace?

**MARGARITA**

All quiet, goor friendsheep; ey mooch a-do, ey strive wid him, give goor worda for you. No more speak a de matra, all es undone, u no more trobla.

Enter **RACHEL** and **KNAVESBEE**.

**CHAMLET** [Giving her money]
Look, there's the price of a fair pair of gloves, and wear 'em for my sake.

**RACHEL**
Oh, oh, oh, my heart's broke out of my ribs!

**KNAVESBEE**
Nay, a little patience.

**MARGARITA**
Ey tank u artely, shall no bestow en gloves; shall put moosh more to dees, an bestow your shop. Regard dess stof a my petticoat. U no soosh anodre; shall deal wid u for moosh: take in your hand.

**CHAMLET**
I see it, mistress; 'tis good stuff indeed. 'Tis a silk rash; I can pattern it.

**RACHEL**
Shall he take up her coats before my face? Oh, beastly creature!

[Coming forward

French hood, French hood, I will make your hair grow thorough!

**CHAMLET**
My wife returned! Oh, welcome home, sweet Rachel!

**RACHEL**
I forbid the banes, lecher! And strumpet, thou shalt bear children without noses!

[She beats **MARGARITA**.

**MARGARITA**
O pardonnez-moi, by my trat ey mean u no hurta! Wat u meant by dees?

**RACHEL**
I will have thine eyes out, and thy bastards shall be as blind as puppies!

**CHAMLET**
Sweet Rachel! Good cousin, help to pacify.

**RACHEL**
I forbid the banes, adulterer!

**CHAMLET**
What means she by that, sir?

**KNAVESBEE** [Restraining her]
Good cousin, forbid your rage a while; unless you hear, by what sense will you receive satisfaction?

**RACHEL**
By my hands and my teeth, sir, give me leave! Will you bind me whiles mine enemy kills me?

**CHAMLET**
Here all are your friends, sweet wife.

**RACHEL**
Wilt have two wives? Do and be hang'd, fornicator! I forbid the banes! Give me the French hood; I'll tread it under feet in a pair of pantofles!

**MARGARITA**
Begar, shall save hood, head, and all; shall come no more heer, ey warran u.

[Exit **MARGARITA**.

**KNAVESBEE**
Sir, the truth is, report spoke it for truth
You were tomorrow to be married.

**RACHEL**
I forbid the banes!

**CHAMLET**
Mercy deliver me,
If my grave embrace me in the bed of death,
I would to church with willing ceremony;
But for my wedlock-fellow, here she is:
The first and last that e'er my thoughts look'd on.

**KNAVESBEE**
Why, la, you, cousin! This was nought but error or an assault of mischief.

**CHAMLET**
Whose report was it?

**KNAVESBEE**
Your man George's, who invited me to the wedding.

[Enter **GEORGE**.

**CHAMLET**
George? And was he sober? Good sir, call him.

**GEORGE**
It needs not, sir; I am here already.

**CHAMLET**
Did you report this, George?

**GEORGE**
Yes, sir, I did.

**CHAMLET**
And wherefore did you so?

**GEORGE**
For a new suit that you promised me, sir, if I could bring home my mistress; and I think she's come, with a mischief.

**RACHEL**
Give me that villain's ears!

**GEORGE**
I would give ear, if I could hear you talk wisely.

**RACHEL**
Let me cut off his ears!

**GEORGE**
I shall hear worse of you hereafter then; limb for limb, one of my ears for one of your tongues, and I'll lay out for my master.

**CHAMLET**
'Twas knavery with a good purpose in't;
Sweet Rachel, this was e'en George's meaning:
A second marriage, 'twixt thyself and me.
And now I woo thee to't; a quiet night
Will make the sun, like a fresh bridegroom, rise
And kiss the chaste cheek of the rosy morn
Which we will imitate, and like him create
Fresh buds of love, fresh spreading arms, fresh fruit,
Fresh wedding robes, and George's fresh new suit.

**RACHEL**
This is fine stuff; have you much on't to see?

**GEORGE**
A remnant of a yard.

**CHAMLET**

Come, come, all's well.
Sir, you must sup, instead of tomorrow's dinner.

**KNAVESBEE**
I follow you.

[Exeunt all but **KNAVESBEE**.

No, 'tis another way;
My lord's reward calls me to better cheer:
Many good meals, a hundred marks a year.
My wife's transform'd a lady. Tush, she'll come
To her shape again; my lord rides the circuit:
If I ride along with him, what need I grutch?
I can as easy, sir, and speed as much.

[Exit **KNAVESBEE**.


ACT V

SCENE I - Before Sir Francis's House

Enter **OLD FRANKLIN** in mourning, young **CRESSINGHAM** with **YOUNG FRANKLIN** disguis'd like an old serving-man.

**CRESSINGHAM**
Sir, your son's death, which has apparell'd you
In this darker wearing, is a loss wherein
I have ample share: he was my friend.

**OLD FRANKLIN**
He was my nearest and dearest enemy,
And the perpetual fear of a worse end,
Had he continued his former dissolute course,
Makes me weigh his death the lighter.

**CRESSINGHAM**
Yet, sir,
With your pardon, if you value him every way
As he deserv'd, it will appear your scanting
Of his means, and the Lord Beaufort's most
Unlordly breach of promise to him, made
Him fall upon some courses, to which his nature
And mine own, made desperate likewise by the cruelty
Of a mother-in-law, would else have been as strange
As insolent greatness is to distress'd virtue.

**OLD FRANKLIN**
Yes, I have heard of that too, your defeat
Made upon a mercer: I style 't modestly,
The law intends it plain cozenage.

**CRESSINGHAM**
'Twas no less,
But my penitence and restitution may
Come fairly off from't: it was no impeachment
To the glory won at Agincourt's great battle
That the achiever of it in his youth
Had been a purse-taker; this with all reverence
To th' great example. Now to my business,
Wherein you have made such noble trial of
Your worth, that in a world so dull as this,
Where faith is almost grown to be a miracle,
I have found a friend so worthy as yourself
To purchase all the land my father sold
At the persuasion of a riotous woman,
And charitable to reserve it for his use
And the good of his three children; this I say
Is such a deed shall style you our preserver,
And owe the memory of your worth, and pay it
To all posterity.

**OLD FRANKLIN**
Sir, what I have done
Looks to the end of the good deed itself,
No other way i' th' world.

**CRESSINGHAM**
But would you please
Out of a friendly reprehension
To make him sensible of the weighty wrong
He has done his children? Yet I would not have it
Too bitter, for he undergoes already
Such torment in a woman's naughty pride,
Too harsh reproof would kill him.

**OLD FRANKLIN**
Leave you that
To my discretion: I have made myself
My son's executor, and am come up
On purpose to collect his creditors,
And where I find his pennyworth conscionable,
I'll make them in part satisfaction.

[Enter **GEORGE**.

Oh, this fellow was born near me, and his trading here i' th' city may bring me to the knowledge of the men my son ought money to.

**GEORGE**
Your worship's welcome to London. And I pray, how does all our good friends i' th' country?

**OLD FRANKLIN**
They are well, George. How thou art shot up since I saw thee! What, I think thou art almost out of thy time?

**GEORGE**
I am out of my wits, sir; I have liv'd in a kind of Bedlam these four years: how can I be mine own man then?

**OLD FRANKLIN**
Why, what's the matter?

**GEORGE**
I may turn soap-boiler, I have a loose body: I am turn'd away from my master.

**OLD FRANKLIN**
How! Turn'd away?

**GEORGE**
I am gone, sir, not in drink, and yet you may behold my indentures.

[He shows his indenture.

Oh, the wicked wit of woman! For the good turn I did bringing her home, she ne'er left sucking my master's breath like a cat, kissing him, I mean, till I was turn'd away!

**OLD FRANKLIN**
I have heard she's a terrible woman.

**GEORGE**
Yes, and the miserablest! Her sparing in housekeeping has cost him somewhat, the Dagger-pies can testify. She has stood in's light most miserably, like your fasting days before red letters in the almanac; saying, the pinching of our bellies would be a mean to make him wear scarlet the sooner. She had once persuaded him to have bought spectacles for all his servants, that they might have worn 'em dinner and supper.

**OLD FRANKLIN**
To what purpose?

**GEORGE**

Marry, to have made our victuals seem bigger than 'twas. She shows from whence she came; that my wind-colic can witness.

**OLD FRANKLIN**
Why, whence came she?

**GEORGE**
Marry, from a courtier, and an officer too, that was up and down I know not how often.

**OLD FRANKLIN**
Had he any great place?

**GEORGE**
Yes, a very high one, but he got little by it; he was one that blew the organ in the court chapel: our puritans, especially your puritans in Scotland, could ne'er away with him.

**OLD FRANKLIN**
Is she one of the sect?

**GEORGE**
Faith, I think not, for I am certain she denies her husband the supremacy.

**OLD FRANKLIN**
Well, George, your difference may be reconcil'd. I am now to use your help in a business that concerns me: here's a note of men's names here i' th' city unto whom my son ought money, but I do not know their dwelling.

**GEORGE** [Taking the note from him]
Let me see, sir. [Reading] "Fifty pound ta'en up at use of Master Waterthin the brewer."

**OLD FRANKLIN**
What's he?

**GEORGE**
An obstinate fellow, and one that denied payment of the groats till he lay by th' heels for't; I know him. [Reading] "Item, fourscore pair of provant breeches a' th' new fashion, to Pinchbuttock, a hosier in Birchen Lane, so much."

**OLD FRANKLIN**
What the devil did he with so many pair of breeches?

**FRANKLIN**
Supply a captain, sir; a friend of his went over to the Palatinate.

**GEORGE** [Reading]
"Item, to my tailor Master Weatherwise, by St. Clement's church."

**CRESSINGHAM**

Who should that be? It may be 'tis the new prophet, the astrological tailor.

**FRANKLIN**
No, no, no, sir; we have nothing to do with him.

**GEORGE**
Well, I'll read no further; leave the note to my discretion: do not fear but I'll inquire them all.

**OLD FRANKLIN**
Why, I thank thee, George. [To **CRESSINGHAM**] Sir, rest assur'd I shall in all your business be faithful to you, and at better leisure find time to imprint deeply in your father the wrong he has done you.

**CRESSINGHAM**
You are worthy in all things.

[Exeunt **OLD FRANKLIN**, **GEORGE** and **YOUNG FRANKLIN**. Enter **SAUNDER**.

Is my father stirring?

**SAUNDER**
Yes, sir. My lady wonders you are thus chargeable to your father, and will not direct yourself unto some gainful study may quit him of your dependence.

**CRESSINGHAM**
What study?

**SAUNDER**
Why, the law, that law that takes up most a' th' wits i' th' kingdom, not for most good, but most gain. Or divinity: I have heard you talk well, and I do not think but you'd prove a singular fine churchman.

**CRESSINGHAM**
I should prove a plural better, if I could attain to fine benefices.

**SAUNDER**
My lady, now she has money, is studying to do good works. She talk'd last night what a goodly act it was of a countess—Northamptonshire breed, belike, or thereabouts—that to make Coventry a corporation, rode through the city naked, and by daylight.

**CRESSINGHAM**
I do not think but you have ladies living would discover as much in private, to advance but some member of a corporation.

[Enter **SIR FRANCIS CRESSINGHAM**.

**SAUNDER**
Well, sir, your wit is still goring at my lady's projects. Here's your father.

**SIR FRANCIS**

Thou com'st to chide me, hearing how like a ward I am handled since the sale of my land.

**CRESSINGHAM**
No, sir, but to turn your eyes into your own bosom.

**SIR FRANCIS**
Why, I am become my wife's pensioner, am confin'd to a hundred mark a year, t' one suit, and one man to attend me?

**SAUNDER**
And is not that enough for a private gentleman?

**SIR FRANCIS**
Peace, sirrah; there is nothing but knave speaks in thee. And my two poor children must be put forth to prentice!

**CRESSINGHAM**
Ha! To prentice? Sir, I do not come to grieve you,
But to show how wretched your estate was,
That you could not come to see order
Until foul disorder pointed the way to't:
So inconsiderate, yet so fruitful still
Is dotage to beget its own destruction.

**SIR FRANCIS**
Surely I am nothing, and desire to be so.
Pray thee, fellow, entreat her only to be quiet;
I have given her all my estate on that condition.

**SAUNDER**
Yes, sir; her coffers are well lin'd, believe me.

**SIR FRANCIS**
And yet she is not contented; we observe
The moon is ne'er so pleasant and so clear
As when she is at the full.

**CRESSINGHAM**
You did no use
My mother with this observance. You are like
The frogs who, weary of their quiet king,
Consented to the election of the stork,
Who in the end devour'd them.

**SIR FRANCIS**
You may see
How apt man is to forfeit all his judgment
Upon the instant of his fall.

**CRESSINGHAM**
Look up, sir.

**SIR FRANCIS**
O, my heart's broke! Weighty are injuries
That come from an enemy, but those are deadly
That come from a friend, for we see commonly
Those are ta'en most to heart.

[Enter the **LADY CRESSINGHAM**.

She comes.

**CRESSINGHAM**
What a terrible eye she darts on us!

**SIR FRANCIS**
Oh, most natural for lightning to go before the thunder.

**LADY CRESSINGHAM**
What? Are you in council? Are ye levying faction against us?

**SIR FRANCIS**
Good friend!

**LADY CRESSINGHAM**
Sir, sir, pray, come hither. There is winter in your looks, a latter winter. Do you complain to your kindred? I'll make you fear extremely to show you have any cause to fear. Are the bonds seal'd for the six thousand pounds I put forth to use?

**SAUNDER**
Yes, madam.

**LADY CRESSINGHAM**
The bonds were made in my uncle's name?

**SAUNDER**
Yes.

**LADY CRESSINGHAM**
'Tis well.

**SIR FRANCIS**
'Tis strange though.

**LADY CRESSINGHAM**

Nothing strange; you'll think the allowance I have put you to as strange, but your judgment cannot reach the aim I have in't. You were prick'd last year to be high sheriff, and what it would have cost you I understand now. All this charge and the other by the sale of your land, and the money at my dispose, and your pension so small, will settle you in quiet, make you master of a retir'd life. And our great ones may think you a politic man, and that you are aiming at some strange business, having made all over.

**SIR FRANCIS**
I must leave you. Man is never truly awake till he be dead!

[Exeunt **SIR FRANCIS CRESSINGHAM** and **SAUNDER.**

**CRESSINGHAM**
What a dream have you made of my father!

**LADY CRESSINGHAM**
Let him be so, and keep the proper place of dream, his bed, until I raise him.

**CRESSINGHAM**
Raise him! Not likely! 'Tis you have ruin'd him!

**LADY CRESSINGHAM**
You do not come to quarrel?

**CRESSINGHAM**
No, certain, but to persuade you to a thing that in the virtue of it nobly carries its own commendation, and you shall gain much honour by it, which is the recompense of all virtuous actions: to use my father kindly.

**LADY CRESSINGHAM**
Why? Does he complain to you, sir?

**CRESSINGHAM**
Complain? Why should a king complain for anything but for his sins to heaven? The prerogative of husband is like to his over his wife.

**LADY CRESSINGHAM**
I am full of business, sir, and will not mind you.

**CRESSINGHAM**
I must not leave you thus; I tell you, mother,
'Tis dangerous to a woman: when her mind
Raises her to such height, it makes her only
Capable of her own merit, nothing of duty!
Oh, 'twas a strange unfortunate o'erprising
Your beauty brought him, otherwise discreet,
Into the fatal neglect of his poor children.
What will you give us of the late sum you receiv'd?

**LADY CRESSINGHAM**
Not a penny. Away, you are troublesome and saucy!

**CRESSINGHAM**
You are too cruel; denials even from princes,
Who may do what they list, should be supplied
With a gracious verbal usage, that though they
Do not cure the sore, they may abate the sense of't.
The wealth you seem to command over is his,
And he I hope will dispose of't to our use.

**LADY CRESSINGHAM**
When he can command my will.

**CRESSINGHAM**
Have you made him
So miserable that he must take a law from his wife?

**LADY CRESSINGHAM**
Have you not had some lawyers forc'd to groan
Under the burden?

**CRESSINGHAM**
Oh, but the greater the women
The more visible are their vices.

**LADY CRESSINGHAM**
So,
Sir, you have been so bold. By all can bind
An oath, and I'll not break it, I will not be
The woman to you hereafter you expected.

**CRESSINGHAM**
Be not; be not yourself, be not my father's wife,
Be not my Lady Cressingham, and then
I'll thus speak to you, but you must not answer
In your own person.

**LADY CRESSINGHAM**
A fine puppet-play!

**CRESSINGHAM**
Good madam, please you pity the mistress
Of a poor gentleman that is undone
By a cruel mother-in-law; you do not know her,
Nor does she deserve the knowledge of any good one,
For she does not know herself. You would sigh for
That e'er she took your sex, if you but heard

Her qualities.

**LADY CRESSINGHAM**
This is a fine crotchet.

**CRESSINGHAM**
Envy and pride flow in her painted breasts,
She gives no other suck; all her attendants
Do not belong to her husband, his money is hers:
Marry, his debts are his own. She bears such sway
She will not suffer his religion be his own
But what she please to turn it to.

**LADY CRESSINGHAM**
And all this while,
I am the woman you libel against.

**CRESSINGHAM**
I remember
Ere the land was sold you talk'd of going to Ireland,
But should you touch there, you would die presently.

**LADY CRESSINGHAM**
Why, man?

**CRESSINGHAM**
The country brooks no poison: go,
You'll find how difficult a thing it is
To make a settled or assur'd estate
Of things ill-gotten. When my father's dead,
The curse of lust and riot follow you!
Marry some young gallant that may rifle you,
Yet add one blessing to your needy age,
That you may die full of repentance.

**LADY CRESSINGHAM**
Ha, ha, ha!

**CRESSINGHAM**
Oh, she is lost to any kind of goodness!

[Exeunt.


SCENE II - A Street Outside Lord Beaufort's House

Enter **LORD BEAUFORT** and **KNAVESBEE**.

**BEAUFORT**
Sirrah, be gone; y'are base!

**KNAVESBEE**
Base, my good lord?
'Tis a ground part in music: trebles, means,
All is but fiddling. Your honour bore a part
As my wife says, my lord.

**BEAUFORT**
Your wife's a strumpet!

**KNAVESBEE**
Ah ha, is she so? I am glad to hear it:
Open confession, open payment.
The wager's mine then, a hundred a year, my lord;
I said so before, and stak'd my head against it.
Thus after darksome night, the day is come, my lord.

**BEAUFORT**
Hence, hide thy branded head; let no day see thee,
Nor thou any but thy execution day!

**KNAVESBEE**
That's the day after washing day; once a week
I see't at home, my lord.

**BEAUFORT**
Go home and see
Thy prostituted wife, for sure 'tis so,
Now folded in a boy's adultery,
My page, on whom the hot-rein'd harlot dotes.
This night he hath been her attendant. My house
He's fled from, and must no more return. Go,
And make haste, sir, lest your reward be lost
For want of looking to.

**KNAVESBEE**
My reward lost!
Is there nothing due for what is past, my lord?

**BEAUFORT** [Beating him]
Yes, pander, wittol, macrio, basest of knaves!
Thou bolster-bawd to thine own infamy!
Go, I have no more about me at this time;
When I am better stor'd thou shalt have more
Where'er I meet thee.

**KNAVESBEE** [Aside]

Pander, wittol, macrio, base knave, bolster-bawd! Here is but five mark toward a hundred a year; this is poor payment. If lords may be trusted no better than thus, I will go home and cut my wife's nose off. I will turn over a new leaf and hang up the page. Lastly, I will put on a large pair of wet-leather boots and drown myself; I will sink at Queenhive and rise again at Charing Cross, contrary to the statute in Edwardo primo.

[Exit. Enter **OLD FRANKLIN**, his son **YOUNG FRANKLIN** - disguised as before, **GEORGE**, three or four citizens as **CREDITORS**.

**OLD FRANKLIN**

Good health to your lordship.

**BEAUFORT**

Master Franklin, I heard of your arrival and the cause of this your sad appearance.

**OLD FRANKLIN**

And 'tis no more than as your honour says, indeed, appearance: it has more form than feeling sorrow, sir, I must confess. There's none of these gentlemen, though aliens in bonds, but have as large cause of grief as I.

**FIRST CREDITOR**

No, by your favour, sir, we are well satisfied. There was in his life a greater hope, but less assurance.

**SECOND CREDITOR**

Sir, I wish all my debts of no better promise to pay me thus; fifty in the hundred comes fairly homewards.

**FRANKLIN**

Considering hard bargains and dead commodities, sir.

**SECOND CREDITOR**

Thou sayst true, friend, and from a dead debtor too.

**BEAUFORT**

And so you have compounded and agreed all your son's riotous debts?

**OLD FRANKLIN**

That's behind but one cause of worse condition; that done, he may sleep quietly.

**FIRST CREDITOR**

Yes, sure, my lord, this gentleman is come a wonder to us all, that so fairly with half a loss could satisfy those debts were dead, even with his son, and from whom we could have nothing claim'd.

**OLD FRANKLIN**

I showed my reason; I would have a good name live after him because he bore my name.

**SECOND CREDITOR**

May his tongue perish first, and that will spoil his trade, that first gives him a syllable of ill.

**BEAUFORT**
Why, this is friendly.

[Enter **CHAMLET**.

**CHAMLET**
My lord!

**BEAUFORT**
Master Chamlet, very welcome.

**CHAMLET**
Master Franklin, I take it. These gentlemen I know well: good Pennystone, Master Phillip, Master Cheyney! I am glad I shall take my leave of so many of my good friends at once.

[Shaking their hands]

Your hand first, my lord; fare you well, sir. Nay, I must have all your hands to my pass.

**GEORGE**
Will you have mine too, sir?

**CHAMLET**
Yes, thy two hands, George, and I think two honest hands of a tradesman, George, as any between Cornhill and Lombard Street.

**GEORGE**
Take heed what you say, sir; there's Birchen Lane between 'em.

**BEAUFORT**
But what's the cause of this, Master Chamlet?

**CHAMLET**
I have the cause in handling now, my lord: George, honest George is the cause, yet no cause of George's. George is turn'd away one way, and I must go another.

**BEAUFORT**
And whither is your way, sir?

**CHAMLET**
E'en to seek out a quiet life, my lord: I do hear of a fine peaceable island.

**BEAUFORT**
Why, 'tis the same you live in.

**CHAMLET**

No, 'tis so fam'd,
But we th' inhabitants find it not so.
The place I speak of has been keep with thunder,
With frightful lightnings, amazing noises,
But now, th' enchantment broke, 'tis the land of peace,
Where hogs and tobacco yield fair increase.

**BEAUFORT**
This is a little wild, methinks.

**CHAMLET**
Gentlemen, fare you well; I am for the Bermudas.

**BEAUFORT**
Nay, good sir, stay. And is that your only cause, the loss of George?

**CHAMLET**
The loss of George, my lord! Make you that no cause? Why, but examine, would it not break the stout heart of a nobleman to lose his George, much more the tender bosom of a citizen?

**BEAUFORT**
Fie, fie, I'm sorry your gravity should run back to lightness thus. You go to the Bermothes!

**OLD FRANKLIN**
Better to Ireland, sir.

**CHAMLET**
The land of ire? That's too near home; my wife will be heard from Hellbree to Divelin.

**OLD FRANKLIN**
Sir, I must of necessity a while detain you. I must acquaint you with a benefit that's coming towards you. You were cheated of some goods of late; come, I'm a cunning man and will help you to the most part again, or some reasonable satisfaction.

**CHAMLET**
That's another cause of my unquiet life, sir. Can you do that, I may chance stay another tide or two.

Enter **RACHEL**.

My wife! I must speak more private with you. By forty foot, pain of death, I dare not reach her. No words of me, sweet gentlemen!

[Slips behind the arras.

**GEORGE**
I had need hide too.

[He follows **CHAMLET**.

**RACHEL**
Oh, my lord, I have scarce tongue enough yet to tell you; my husband, my husband's gone from me. Your warrant, good my lord, I never had such need of your warrant; my husband's gone from me!

**BEAUFORT**
Going he is, 'tis true; h'as ta'en his leave of me, and all these gentlemen, and 'tis your sharp tongue that whips him forward.

**RACHEL**
A warrant, good my lord!

**BEAUFORT**
You turn away his servants, such on whom his estate depends, he says, who know his books, his debts, his customers; the form and order of all his affairs you make orderless. Chiefly, his George you have banish'd from him.

**RACHEL**
My lord, I will call George again.

**GEORGE** [within]
Call George again!

**BEAUFORT**
Why, hark you, how high-voic'd you are that raise an echo from my cellarage, which we with modest loudness cannot.

**RACHEL**
My lord, do you think I speak too loud?

**GEORGE** within
Too loud.

**BEAUFORT**
Why hark, your own tongue answers you, and reverberates your words into your teeth.

**RACHEL**
I will speak lower all the days of my life: I never found the fault in myself till now. Your warrant, good my lord, to stay my husband!

**BEAUFORT**
Well, well, it shall o'ertake him ere he pass Gravesend, provided that he meet his quietness at home; else, he's gone again.

**OLD FRANKLIN**
And withal to call George again.

**RACHEL**

I will call George again.

**GEORGE** within
Call George again.

**BEAUFORT**
See, you are raised again, the echo tells you.

**RACHEL**
I did forget myself indeed, my lord: this is my last fault; I will go make a silent inquiry after George. I will whisper half a score porters in the ear that shall run softly up and down the city to seek him. Be wi' ye, my lord; bye all, gentlemen.

[Exit. **CHAMLET** and **GEORGE** come forward.]

**BEAUFORT**
George, your way lies before you now: cross the street and come into her eyes; your master's journey will be stay'd.

**GEORGE**
I'll warrant you bring it to better subjection yet.

[Exit.

**BEAUFORT**
These are fine flashes; how now, Master Chamlet?

**CHAMLET**
I had one ear lent to you-ward, my lord,
And this o' th' tother side; both sounded sweetly:
I have whole recovered my late losses, sir;
Th'one half paid, the tother is forgiven.

**BEAUFORT**
Then your journey is stay'd?

**CHAMLET**
Alas, my lord,
That was a trick of age, for I had left
Never a trick of youth like it to succour me.

[Enter **BARBER** and **KNAVESBEE**.

**BEAUFORT**
How now? What new object's here?

**BARBER** [To **KNAVESBEE**]
The next man we meet shall judge us.

**KNAVESBEE** [To **BARBER**]
Content, though he be but a common councilman.

**BEAUFORT**
The one's a knave; I could know him at twelvescore distance.

**OLD FRANKLIN**
And tother's a barber-surgeon, my lord.

**KNAVESBEE**
I'll go no further; here is the honourable lord that I know will grant my request. My lord—

**BARBER**
Peace, I will make it plain to his lordship. My lord, a covenant by jus jurandum is between us: he is to suffocate my respiration by his capistrum, and I to make incision so far as mortification by his jugulars.

**BEAUFORT**
This is not altogether so plain neither, sir.

**BARBER**
I can speak no plainer, my lord, unless I wrong mine art.

**KNAVESBEE**
I can, my lord; I know some part of the law. I am to take him in this place where I find him, and lead him from hence to the place of execution, and there to hang him till he dies. He in equal courtesy is to cut my throat with his razor, and there's an end of both on's.

**BARBER**
There is the end, my lord, but we want the beginning. I stand upon it to be strangled first before I touch either his gula or cervix.

**KNAVESBEE**
I am against it, for how shall I be sure to have my throat cut after he's hang'd?

**BEAUFORT**
Is this a condition betwixt you?

**KNAVESBEE**
A firm covenant, sign'd and seal'd by oath and handfast, and wants nothing but agreement.

**BEAUFORT**
A little pause: what might be the cause on either part?

**BARBER**
My passions are grown to putrefaction, and my griefs are gangren'd; Master Chamlet has scarified me all over, besides the loss of my new brush.

**KNAVESBEE**

I am kept out of mine own castle; my wife keeps the hold against me. Your page, my lord, is her champion; I summon'd a parle at the window, was answered with defiance. They confess they have lain together, but what they have done else I know not.

**BEAUFORT**

Thou canst have no wrong that deserves pity, thou art thyself so bad.

**KNAVESBEE**

I thank your honour for that; let me have my throat cut then.

**CHAMLET**

Sir, I can give you a better remedy than his capistrum; your ear a little. [Whispers to **BEAUFORT**.]

[Enter **MISTRESS CRESSINGHAM** as a woman, and **SIB**.

**SIB**

I come with a bold innocence to answer
The best and worst that can accuse me here.

**BEAUFORT**

Your husband.

**SIB**

He's the worst, I dare his worst.

**KNAVESBEE**

Your page, your page.

**SIB**

We lay together in bed,
It is confess'd; you and your ends of law
Make worser of it: I did it for reward.

**BEAUFORT**

I'll hear no more of this. Come, gentlemen, will you walk?

[Enter young **CRESSINGHAM**.

**CRESSINGHAM**

My lord, a little stay; you'll see a sight
That neighbour amity will be much pleas'd with.
'Tis come already: my father, sir.

[Enter **SIR FRANCIS**, finely dressed].

**BEAUFORT**

There must be cause, certain, for this good change.

Sir, you are bravely met;
This is at the best I ever saw you.

**SIR FRANCIS**
My lord, I am amazement to myself;
I slept in poverty, and am awake
Into this wonder. How I came thus brave,
My dreams did not so much as tell me of.
I am of my kind son's new making up;
It exceeds the pension much that yesternight
Allow'd me, and my pockets centupled,
But I am my son's child, sir: he knows of me
More than I do myself.

**CRESSINGHAM**
Sir, you yet have
But earnest of your happiness, a pinnace
Foreriding a goodly vessel by this near anchor,
Bulk'd like a castle, and with jewels fraught,
Joys above jewels, sir, from deck to keel.
Make way for the receipt, empty your bosom
Of all griefs and troubles, leave not a sigh
To beat her back again; she is so stor'd
Ye'ad need have room enough to take her lading.

**SIR FRANCIS**
If one commodity be wanting now,
All this is nothing.

**CRESSINGHAM**
Tush, that must out too.
There must be no remembrance, not the thought
That ever youth in woman did abuse you,
That e'er your children had a stepmother,
That you sold lands to please your punishment,
That you were circumscrib'd and taken in,
Abridg'd the large extendure of your grounds,
And put into the pinfold that belong'd to't,
That your son did cheat for want of maintenance;
That he did beg, you shall remember only,
For I have begg'd off all these troubles from you.

**BEAUFORT**
This was a good week's labour.

**CRESSINGHAM**
Not an hour's,
My lord, but 'twas a happy one. See, sir,

A new day shines on you.

[Enter **LADY CRESSINGHAM** in civil habit, **SAUNDER**, and children - **MARIA** and **EDWARD** dressed very gallant.

**LADY CRESSINGHAM**
Oh, sir, your son
Has robb'd me!

**SIR FRANCIS**
Ha! That way I instructed?

**CRESSINGHAM**
Nay, hear her, sir.

**LADY CRESSINGHAM**
Of my good purpose, sir;
He hath forc'd out of me what lay conceal'd,
Ripen'd my pity with his dews of duty.
Forgive me, sir, and but keep the number
Of every grief that I have pain'd you with;
I'll tenfold pay with fresh obedience.

**CHAMLET**
Oh, that my wife were here to learn this lesson!

**LADY CRESSINGHAM**
Your state is not abated; what was yours
Is still your own, and take the cause withal
Of my harsh-seeming usage. It was to reclaim
Faults in yourself, the swift consumption
Of many large revenues, gaming, that
Of not much less speed, burning up house and land,
Not casual but cunning fire, which though
It keeps the chimney and outward shows
Like hospitality, is only devourer on't,
Consuming chemistry. There I have made you
A flat bankrout; all your stillatories
And labouring minerals are demolish'd:
That part of hell in your house is extinct.
Put out your desire with them, and then these feet
Shall level with my hands, until you raise
My stoop'd humility to higher grace,
To warm these lips with love and duty do
To every silver hair: each one shall be
A senator to my obedience.

**SIR FRANCIS**

All this I knew before: whoever of you
That had but one ill thought of this good woman,
You owe a knee to her, and she is merciful
If she forgive you.

**BEAUFORT**
That shall be private penance, sir; we'll joy in public with you.

[Enter **GEORGE** and **RACHEL**.

**GEORGE**
On the conditions I tell you, not else.

**RACHEL**
Sweet George, dear George, any conditions.

**CHAMLET** ·
My wife!

**OLD FRANKLIN**
Peace, George is bringing her to conditions.

**CHAMLET**
Good ones, good George.

**GEORGE**
You shall never talk your voice above the key sol, sol, sol.

**RACHEL**
Sol, sol, sol; ay, George.

**GEORGE**
Say, "Welcome home, honest George," in that pitch.

**RACHEL**
Welcome home, honest George.

**GEORGE**
Why, this is well now.

**CHAMLET**
That's well indeed, George.

**GEORGE**
"Rogue" nor "rascal" must never come out of your mouth.

**RACHEL**
They shall never come in, honest George.

**GEORGE**
Nor I will not have you call my master plain husband, that's too coarse; but as your gentlewomen in the country use and your parsons' wives in the town, 'tis comely and shall be customed in the city, call him Master Chamlet at every word.

**RACHEL**
At every word, honest George.

**GEORGE**
Look you, there he is: salute him then.

**RACHEL**
Welcome home, good Master Chamlet.

**CHAMLET**
Thanks and a thousand, sweet. "Wife," I may say, honest George?

**GEORGE**
Yes, sir, or "bird," or "chuck," or "heart's ease," or plain "Rachel;" but call her "Rac" no more, as long as she is quiet.

**CHAMLET**
God-a-mercy, sha't have thy new suit a' Sunday, George.

**RACHEL**
George shall have two new suits, Master Chamlet.

**CHAMLET**
God-a-mercy, i'faith, chuck!

**BARBER**
Master Chamlet, you and I are friends, all even betwixt us?

**CHAMLET**
I do acquit thee, neighbour Sweetball.

**BARBER**
I will not be hang'd then; Knavesbee, do thy worst, nor I will not cut thy throat.

**KNAVESBEE**
I must do't myself.

**BARBER**
If thou com'st to my shop and usurp'st my chair of maintenance, I will go as near as I can, but I will not do't.

**CRESSINGHAM**

No, 'tis I must cut Knavesbee's throat, for slandering a modest gentlewoman, and my wife, in the shape of your page, my lord. In her own I durst not place her so near your lordship.

**BEAUFORT**
No more of that, sir; if your ends have acquir'd their own events, crown 'em with your own joy.

**CRESSINGHAM**
Down a' your knees, Knavesbee, to your wife: she's too honest for you.

**BARBER**
Down, down, before you are hang'd; 'twill be too late afterwards, and long thou canst not 'scape it.

[**KNAVESBEE** kneels and **SIB** holds the Barber's razor to his throat].

**SIB**
You'll play the pander no more, will you?

**KNAVESBEE**
Oh, that's an inch into my throat!

**SIB**
And let out your wife for hire?

**KNAVESBEE**
Oh sweet wife, go no deeper!

**SIB**
Dare any be bail for your better behaviour?

**BEAUFORT**
Yes, yes, I dare; he will mend one day.

**SIB**
And be worse the next.

**KNAVESBEE**
Hang me the third then, dear merciful wife;
I will do anything for a quiet life!

**BEAUFORT**
All then is reconcil'd.

**BARBER**
Only my brush is lost. My dear new brush!

**OLD FRANKLIN**
I will help you to satisfaction for that too, sir.

**BARBER**
Oh, spermaceti, I feel it heal already!

**OLD FRANKLIN**
Gentlemen, I have fully satisfied my dead son's debts?

**CREDITORS**
All pleas'd, all paid, sir.

**OLD FRANKLIN**
Then once more here I bring him back to life:
From my servant to my son.

[He removes **FRANKLIN'S** disguise.]

Nay, wonder not.
I have not dealt by fallacy with any;
My son was dead: whoe'er outlives his virtues
Is a dead man, for when you hear of spirits
That walk in real bodies to the amaze
And cold astonishment of such as meet 'em
And all would shun, those are men of vices,
Who nothing have but what is visible,
And so by consequence they have no souls.
But if the soul return, he lives again,
Created newly; such my son appears,
By my blessing rooted, growing by his tears.

**CREDITORS**
You have beguil'd us honestly, sir.

**FRANKLIN**
And you shall have your brush again.

**BARBER**
My basins shall all ring for joy.

**BEAUFORT**
Why, this deserves a triumph, and my cost
Shall begin a feast to't, to which I do
Invite you all. Such happy reconcilements
Must not be past without a health of joy:
Discorded friends aton'd, men and their wives,
This hope proclaims your after quiet lives.

[Exeunt.

I am sent t'inquire your censure, and to know
How you stand affected; [whether] we do owe
Our service to your favours, or must strike
Our sails, though full of hope, to your dislike.
Howe'er, be pleas'd to think we purpos'd well,
And from my fellows thus much I must tell:
Instruct us but in what we went astray,
And to redeem it, we'll take any way.


## Thomas Middleton – A Short Biography

Thomas Middleton was born in London in April 1580 and baptised on 18th April. He was the son of a bricklayer who had raised himself to the status of a gentleman and become the owner of property adjoining the Curtain Theatre in Shoreditch.

Middleton was aged only five when his father died. His mother remarried but this new union unfortunately fell apart and turned into a fifteen year legal conflict centered on the inheritance of Thomas and his younger sister.

Middleton went on to attend Queen's College, Oxford, matriculating in 1598. However he failed to graduate for reasons unknown leaving either in 1600 or 1601. He had by that time written and published three long poems in popular Elizabethan styles. None appears to have been commercially successful although Microcynicon: Six Snarling Satirese was denounced by the Archbishop of Canterbury and publicly burned as part of his attack on verse satire. Although a minor work, the poems show the roots of Middleton's interest in, and later mature work on, sin, hypocrisy, and lust.

In the early years of the 17th century, Middleton made a living writing topical pamphlets, including one, Penniless Parliament of Threadbare Poets, that was reprinted several times as well as becoming the subject of a parliamentary inquiry.

For one so young he was already making quite an impact and had obviously attracted the eye of the authorities in those turbulent times.

Records surviving of the great theatrical entrepreneur of the day, Philip Henslowe, confirm that Middleton was writing for Henslowe's Admiral's Men. His lauded contemporary, a certain William Shakespeare, was writing only for Henslowe whereas Middleton remained a free agent and able to write for whichever theatrical company hired him.

These early years writing plays continued to attract controversy. His friendship and writing partnership with Thomas Dekker brought him into conflict with Ben Jonson and George Chapman in the so-called War of the Theatres. (This controversy was also called the Poetomachia by Thomas Dekker. The Bishops Ban of 1599 had removed any use of satire from prose and verse publications and so the only outlet was on the stage. For the next 3 years Ben Jonson and George Chapman on one side and John Marston,

Thomas Dekker and Thomas Middleton on the other poked fun at their opposition with characters from their plays. The grudge against Jonson continued as late as 1626, when Jonson's play The Staple of News indulges in a slur on Middleton's last play, A Game at Chess).

In 1603, Middleton married. It was also a momentous year in other respects. On the death of Elizabeth I, her cousin James VI of Scotland was now also crowned King James I of England. Another outbreak of the plague now forced the theatres in London to close.

For Middleton the changeover from Elizabethan to Jacobean was the beginning of a long period of success as a writer.

When the theatres re-opened and welcomed back audiences in need of entertainment Middleton was there, writing for several different companies. In particular he specialised in city comedy and revenge tragedy.

During this time he appears also to have written with Shakespeare and he is variously attributed as collaborating on All's Well That Ends Well and Timon of Athens.

Although Middleton had started as a junior partner to Thomas Dekker he was now his fully fledged equal. His finest work with Dekker was undoubtedly The Roaring Girl, a biography of the notorious contemporary thief Mary Frith (Frith began her criminal career as a pickpocket before moving on to highway robbery with a penchant for dressing up as a man. A spell in prison was followed by a long career as a 'fence' from her shop in Fleet St. She lived to the then quite extraordinary age of 74.) The writing is noteworthy not only for its playwriting ambition but in producing a fully formed heroine in Moll Cutpurse. This was only shortly after the role of women in plays had seen fit to have them played, in the main, by men.

In the 1610s, Middleton began another playwriting partnership, this time with the actor William Rowley, producing another slew of plays including the classics Wit at Several Weapons and A Fair Quarrel.

The ever adaptable Middleton seemed at ease working with others or by himself. His solo writing credits include the comic masterpiece, A Chaste Maid in Cheapside, in 1613. Interestingly his solo plays are somewhat less thrusting and bellicose. Certainly there is no comedy among them with the satirical depth of Michaelmas Term and no tragedy as raw, striking and as bloodthirsty as The Revenger's Tragedy.

There may be various reasons for this and among them that he was increasingly involved with civic pageants and therefore was trying to avoid too much controversy especially without the cover of a collaborator. Indeed in 1620, he was officially appointed as chronologer of the City of London, a post he held until his death in 1627, when ironically, it passed to his great rival, and sometime enemy, Ben Jonson.

Middleton's official duties did not interrupt his dramatic writing; the 1620s saw the production of his and Rowley's tragedy, and continual favourite, The Changeling, as well as several other tragicomedies.

However in 1624, he reached a peak of notoriety when his dramatic allegory A Game at Chess was staged by the King's Men. The play used the conceit of a chess game to present and satirise the recent intrigues surrounding the Spanish Match; James I's son, Prince Charles, was being positioned to marry the daughter, Maria Anna of the Spanish King Philip IV of Spain. Though Middleton's approach was strongly patriotic, the Privy Council closed the play, after only nine performances at the Globe theatre, having received a complaint from the Spanish ambassador. The Privy Council then opened a prosecution against both authors and actors. Although Middleton in his defence showed that the play had been passed by the Master of the Revels, Sir Henry Herbert, any further performance was forbidden and the author and actors fined.

What happened next is a mystery. It is the last play recorded as having being written by Middleton. His playwriting career appears to have stopped dead. It follows that some sort of further punishment probably occurred and for a writer can there be any greater punishment than not being allowed to write or be heard?

Middleton's work is diverse even by the standards of his age. His career Middleton covers many many genres including tragedy, history and city comedy. As we have noted he did not have the kind of official relationship with a particular company that Shakespeare or Fletcher had that might have supported him in a lean creative period. Instead he appears to have written on a freelance basis for any number of companies. His output ranges from the "snarling" satire of Michaelmas Term, performed by the Children of Paul's, to the bleak intrigues of The Revenger's Tragedy, performed by the King's Men. Interestingly earlier editions of The Revenger's Tragedy attributed the play solely to Cyril Tourneur but recent studies have shredded that view so that Middleton's authorship is not now seriously contested

Indeed modern techniques in analysing writing styles are now leaning towards giving Middleton credit for his adaptation and revision of Shakespeare's Macbeth and Measure for Measure. Along with the more established evidence of collaboration on All's Well That Ends Well and Timon of Athens it appears that Middleton has moved some way forward to the front rank of playwrights and an association, in some form, but its greatest exponent.

His early work was informed by the blossoming, in the late Elizabethan period, of satire, while his maturity was influenced by the ascendancy of Fletcherian tragicomedy. Middleton's later work, in which his satirical fury is tempered and broadened, includes three of his acknowledged masterpieces. A Chaste Maid in Cheapside, produced by the Lady Elizabeth's Men, which skillfully combines London life with an expansive view of the power of love to effect reconciliation even though London seems populated entirely by sinners, in which no social rank goes unsatirised. The Changeling, a later tragedy, returns Middleton to an Italianate setting like that of The Revenger's Tragedy, except that here the central characters are more fully drawn and more compelling as individuals. Similar development can be seen in Women Beware Women.

Middleton's plays are marked by their cynicism, though often very funny, about the human race. His characters are complex. True heroes are a rarity: almost all of his characters are selfish, greedy, and self-absorbed.

When Middleton does portray good people, the characters are often presented as flawless and perfect and given small, undemanding roles. A theological pamphlet attributed to Middleton gives sustenance to the notion that Middleton was a strong believer in Calvinism.

Thomas Middleton died at his home at Newington Butts in Southwark in the summer of 1627, and was buried on July 4th, in St Mary's churchyard which today survives as a public park in Elephant and Castle.

Middleton stands with John Fletcher and Ben Jonson as the most successful and prolific of playwrights from the Jacobean period. Very few Renaissance dramatists would achieve equal success in both comedy and tragedy but Middleton was one. He also wrote many masques and pageants and remains, to this day, one of the most notable of Jacobean dramatists.

Middleton's work has long been praised by many literary critics, among the most fervent were Algernon Charles Swinburne and T. S. Eliot. The latter thought Middleton was second only to Shakespeare.

Among their contemporaries was a very crowded field of talent including: Ben Jonson (1572-1637), Christopher Marlowe (1564-1593), Francis Beaumont (1585-1616), Henry Chettle (1564-1606), John Fletcher (1579–1625), John Ford (1586–1639), John Day (1574-1640), John Marston (1576-1634), John Webster (1580-1634), Nathan Field (1587-1620), Philip Massinger (1584-1640), Richard Burbage (1567-1619), Robert Greene (1558-1592), Thomas Dekker (1575-1625), Thomas Kyd (1558-1594), William Haughton (died 1605), William Rowley (1585-1626).

It's a daunting list and confirms that to top that made you a very special talent indeed.


Thomas Middleton – A Concise Bibliography

It has long been recognised that the modern concept of authorship was rather more elastic in centuries past. Writers were not only for hire, and their work therefore a commodity, but their plays ran much shorter lengths; two weeks being a common term of performance. To that themes and scenes were liberally excised from one play and used in another. Revisions to past plays that were being restaged would be undertaken and entirely credited to other writers. Many works and plays were unpublished and have not survived and some only from memory by actors etc. Whilst many of these playwrights are only now feted for their talents, some undoubtedly were at the time, but it is difficult to, in every case, to establish exact provenance. With modern scholarly and literary techniques author attributions have sometimes changed or been re-balanced. For those where this may be the case we have placed the *Play's Title and other information* in italics


Plays
Blurt, Master Constable or The Spaniard's Night Walk (with Thomas Dekker (1602)
The Phoenix (1603–4)
The Honest Whore, Part 1, a city comedy (1604), (with Thomas Dekker)
Michaelmas Term, a city comedy, (1604)
*All's Well That Ends Well (1604-5); believed by some to be co-written by Middleton based on stylometric analysis.*
A Trick to Catch the Old One, a city comedy (1605)
A Mad World, My Masters, a city comedy (1605)
*A Yorkshire Tragedy, a one-act tragedy (1605); attributed to Shakespeare on its title page, but stylistic analysis favours Middleton.*
*Timon of Athens a tragedy (1605–6); stylistic analysis indicates that Middleton may have written this play in collaboration with William Shakespeare.*
The Puritan (1606)
The Revenger's Tragedy (1606). Earlier editions often mistakenly attribute authorship to Cyril Tourneur.

Your Five Gallants, a city comedy (1607)
*The Family of Love (1607) some attribute this to Middleton others include Dekker and Lording Barry.*
The Bloody Banquet (1608–9); co-written with Thomas Dekker.
The Roaring Girl, a city comedy depicting the exploits of Mary Frith (1611); with Thomas Dekker.
No Wit, No Help Like a Woman's, a tragic-comedy (1611)
The Second Maiden's Tragedy, a tragedy (1611); an anonymous manuscript; stylistic analysis indicates Middleton's authorship (though one scholar also attributed it to Shakespeare.
A Chaste Maid in Cheapside, a city comedy (1613)
*Wit at Several Weapons*, a city comedy (1613); printed as part of the Beaumont and Fletcher Folio, but stylistic analysis indicates comprehensive revision by Middleton & Rowley.
More Dissemblers Besides Women, a tragicomedy (1614)
The Widow (1615–16)
The Witch, a tragicomedy (1616)
A Fair Quarrel, a tragicomedy (1616). Co-written with William Rowley.
The Old Law, a tragicomedy (1618–19). written with William Rowley and perhaps a third collaborator.
Hengist, King of Kent, or The Mayor of Quinborough, a tragedy (1620)
Women Beware Women, a tragedy (1621)
Measure for Measure (1603-4); some scholars argue that the First Folio text was partly revised by Middleton in 1621.
Anything for a Quiet Life, a city comedy (1621). Co-written with John Webster.
The Changeling, a tragedy (1622). Co-written with William Rowley.
*The Nice Valour* (1622). Printed as part of the Beaumont and Fletcher Folio, but stylistic analysis indicates comprehensive revision by Middleton.
The Spanish Gypsy, a tragicomedy (1623). Believed to be a play by Middleton & Rowley and later revised by Thomas Dekker and John Ford.
A Game at Chess, a political satire (1624). Satirized the negotiations over the proposed marriage of Prince Charles, son of James I of England, with the Spanish princess. Closed after nine performances.


Masques & Entertainments
The Whole Royal and Magnificent Entertainment Given to King James Through the City of London (1603–4). Co-written with Thomas Dekker, Stephen Harrison & Ben Jonson.
The Manner of his Lordship's Entertainment
The Triumphs of Truth
Civitas Amor
The Triumphs of Honour and Industry (1617)
The Masque of Heroes, or, The Inner Temple Masque (1619)
The Triumphs of Love and Antiquity (1619)
The World Tossed at Tennis (1620). Co-written with William Rowley.
Honourable Entertainments (1620–1)
An Invention (1622)
The Sun in Aries (1621)
The Triumphs of Honour and Virtue (1622)
The Triumphs of Integrity with The Triumphs of the Golden Fleece (1623)
The Triumphs of Health and Prosperity (1626)


Poetry

The Wisdom of Solomon Paraphrased (1597)
Microcynicon: Six Snarling Satires (1599)
The Ghost of Lucrece (1600)
Burbage epitaph (1619)
Bolles epitaph (1621)
Duchess of Malfi (commendatory poem) (1623)
St James (1623)
To the King (1624)


Prose
The Penniless Parliament of Threadbare Poets (1601)
News from Gravesend. Co-written with Thomas Dekker (1603)
The Nightingale and the Ant aka Father Hubbard's Tales (1604)
The Meeting of Gallants at an Ordinary (1604). Co-written with Thomas Dekker.
Plato's Cap Cast at the Year 1604 (1604)
The Black Book (1604)
Sir Robert Sherley his Entertainment in Cracovia (1609) (translation).
The Two Gates of Salvation (1609), or The Marriage of the Old and New Testament.
The Owl's Almanac (1618)
The Peacemaker (1618)

www.ingramcontent.com/pod-product-compliance
Lightning Source LLC
Chambersburg PA
CBHW060132050426
42448CB00010B/2079